BARNES & NOBLE
BUSINESS BASICS™

résumés and cover letters

by Susan Stellin

BARNES
& NOBLE
BOOKS
NEW YORK

For information, contact:
Barnes & Noble, Publishing, Inc.
122 Fifth Avenue
New York, NY 10011
212-633-4000

introduction

"Writing a résumé—it should be an easy task," sighed Sam, "but every time I start, I get stuck. Should I mention the marketing responsibilities of my last job if I am applying for a sales position? How do I handle the fact that I took a year off to teach skiing? And posting my résumé on the Internet—what's going to make mine stand out? Finally, cover letters. I have no idea what to say in those. There is just so much to figure out. I don't know where to start."

Relax. You can start right here with **Barnes & Noble Business Basics** *Résumés and Cover Letters*. It walks you through the entire process, explaining the different résumé styles, what you need to know about sending yours electronically, and how to follow up once you've sent it in. It will help you handle such tricky situations as that skiing hiatus; how to market yourself if you are just out of college; what to say if you were fired from your last position; how to write those important cover letters and thank-you notes, and much, much more.

Remember, your résumé is your ticket to getting that job interview. Write a compelling one and your next phone call could be from a job recruiter inviting you in for a chat. Good luck!

Barb Chintz
Editorial Director, the **Barnes & Noble Business Basics**™ series

table of contents

Résumé basics

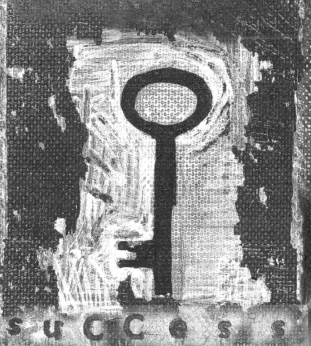

The purpose of a résumé is to get an interview, not a job.

success

what is a résumé for?

Getting your foot
in the door

Alright, you are ready to work on your resume! Good for you. A smart, compelling résumé is often the best way to grab an employer's attention.

"Attention?" you may be thinking. "But I want a job!" Here's a news flash: The whole purpose of your résumé is to get an interview, not magically land you a job offer. Think about it: No employer is going to hire someone based on a one-page document. But if you create a compelling résumé, you have a good shot at landing an interview where you can then talk your way into a job.

Most people think of a résumé as a work-life summary: where they have been employed and how long they held each job. But a good résumé does much more than that; it serves as a marketing and sales tool. Think of your résumé as a book jacket or a movie trailer. It should be a teaser that makes employers want to find out more about you—it doesn't tell the whole story. You want to save that for your interview.

ASK THE EXPERTS

Do I need to know what sort of work I want to do before I write my résumé?

Yes, you do need to have some inkling of the kind of work you want to do. Why? Because shaping your résumé around a work goal will help you get better results, namely more interviews with prospective employers.

How do I figure out what kind of work is best for me and write a résumé with that in mind?

If you're just starting out in the work world or you want to switch careers and you aren't sure what you want to do, consider hiring a career counselor, who can help focus your job search and revise your résumé. Career counselors can help you assess your strengths and weaknesses and match them up with the right career. They can also help you create a résumé that opens the door to new career options. Think of a career counselor as a personal trainer, someone who is part expert, part coach. For more on hiring a counselor see page 24.

résumé nuts and bolts

Help the reader
go through your
résumé one step
at a time

When you sit down to design your résumé, you need to think about how to translate your skills and experiences onto paper. To do that, break your résumé down into three key sections: experience, education, and skills. That done, you can expand your résumé to include other areas of expertise, such as languages and volunteer work. Whether this is your first résumé or your fifteenth, these are the basic categories you will work with. As you build on your skills try to confine your résumé to no more than two pages—one if you have less than 10 years' experience.

Experience
This is the core of your résumé. Writing about your experience in a smart, compelling way is what will distinguish your résumé from others. Consider all your work experience, paid and unpaid. Start with your most recent position. Analyze it according to the abilities and skills you mastered, or by your accomplishments. What do you want to underscore? What do you want to leave out? (More specific information about how to present your experience is on page 40.)

Education
This is more than a list of schools you attended and degrees, certificates, or diplomas you earned. Think through your educational achievements and see what stands out. For example, if you're looking for a technical job, a summary of related college courses is a good idea. Never list a degree you haven't earned. And if you've been out of school for longer than 15 years, leave off the dates of attendance.

Skills
Skills fall into all sorts of categories. They are not hobbies or interests, they are subjects in which you have acquired some degree of mastery. There are computer skills, such as the ability to work in various software programs. There are knowledge skills, such as having a working knowledge of a foreign language. And finally there are life skills, such as cooking well or being an ace skier. Be sure to list only those that you think would impress an employer.

Optional Résumé Sections

Objective

This is one or two sentences stating the kind of job you want. It usually appears at the top of your résumé. It lets an employer know your aim, but it could limit the jobs for which you are considered.

Summary of Qualifications

This brief listing, also at the top of a résumé, highlights your strongest selling points related to the job you want. While not yet standard, qualification summaries (also known as Summary Statements) are becoming more prevalent. Offering a quick preview of your experience, a summary serves to quickly position you in the hiring manager's mind—which can be particularly important if you've held jobs in different fields and need to pull diverse experiences together. However, this information can also be effectively presented in your cover letter (see page 120).

Volunteer Activities

Here's where you can showcase any serious volunteer commitments you've had in your community—coaching a Little League team, organizing an art show at the local museum, reading to the blind, or tutoring disadvantaged students. Volunteer jobs are important because they show that you are building skills that can be applied to a paid job.

Interests

Although job seekers with more experience probably won't want to include a section listing interests, it is more acceptable for recent college graduates or those new to the workforce. Listing interests such as playing the flute, being on the swim team, or singing in a choir can provide conversation starters in an interview, especially if they relate to the job you want.

choosing a résumé format

Chronological vs. functional

The first decision you need to make as you sit down to write your résumé is which format to use. Although several variations have emerged over the years, two basic styles have stood the test of time: the chronological and the functional résumé.

The most common format, the **chronological résumé**, lists a candidate's work experience starting with the most recent job and working backward. (For this reason, it is sometimes referred to as a "reverse chronological" résumé.) Specific achievements are listed below each position, highlighting skills used in the past that are relevant to the job you want.

The second most common format is called a **functional résumé**. Instead of listing each position held, this type of résumé is organized according to various skills you have acquired throughout your career, such as "sales," "project management," or "product development." Specific accomplishments are listed below these skill headings rather than below each job title. But even in a functional résumé, a brief section at the bottom of the page lists past employers and dates of employment.

What is sometimes referred to as a **hybrid résumé** combines features of the chronological and functional formats. For example, you might use the basic template of a chronological résumé but, below each job, list two or three skills you developed in that position (see page 18).

Which One Should I Use?

When to use a chronological résumé

- Your work history has been relatively stable.

- You are applying to a traditional company.

- Your most recent employers or job titles are impressive.

- You aren't sure which format to use.

When to consider a functional résumé

- You have gaps in your employment history.

- You are trying to change careers.

- You have little or no work experience.

- You have had many jobs using similar skills.

- Your most recent work experience is less impressive than past jobs.

When to use a hybrid résumé

- Your previous job titles do not adequately highlight skills necessary for the position you are applying for. (For example, you have a broad title like "program assistant" or "project director," but you want to emphasize your marketing experience.)

- You are changing careers and want to emphasize skills that are important in your new field but may not have been the primary focus of your previous work.

- You like the idea of a functional résumé but are concerned that potential employers would prefer the chronological format.

the chronological résumé

Your experience at a glance

The conventional wisdom is that hiring managers prefer **chronological résumés** because they are easier to read. A chronological résumé reveals a person's entire work history at a glance. If you have a solid track record with few gaps, then the chronological résumé is the way to go.

The good news is that a chronological résumé is fairly easy to write. You simply describe your work history and your education as they happened. It's your own personal timeline. Some chronological résumés use bulleted phrases below each job description rather than a paragraph of text; these are sometimes referred to as **linear résumés** and can be easier for employers to read at a glance.

The one drawback to the chronological résumé is that its format can shift the emphasis from what you want to do now to what you have done in the past and for how long. For this reason, it is important that your descriptions about your duties and accomplishments in each job be compelling, or that you use a Summary of Qualifications to headline the skills and experience you want to emphasize. (See page 188 for ways to revise your résumé.)

A You Say Experience, I Say Work

The Professional Experience section can also be titled Work Experience, Relevant Experience, or even Employment. This section lists each position held, starting with the most recent, and includes the name of the company, your job title, your dates of employment, and a brief description of your accomplishments in the position. You can list the company name or your job title first, depending on which presents you in the strongest light.

Todd Evans
625 Weston Lane, Los Angeles, CA 90046
tevans@webmail.net   213-555-3092

OBJECTIVE: A position as a publicist in the entertainment industry.

SUMMARY OF QUALIFICATIONS

- 9 years' experience in marketing, communications, and public relations for high-profile clients

- Extensive contacts in the music and film industries in Los Angeles and New York

- Avid networker with a gregarious personality, comfortable talking with anyone

PROFESSIONAL EXPERIENCE

2000–present   **Public Relations Manager,** Spotlight Films, Los Angeles, CA

> Manage communications strategy for award-winning film studio, including publicity for upcoming movie release shown at the 2002 Toronto International Film Festival.

> Plan and supervise media events for movie releases, consistently generating positive coverage in national broadcast and print media.

1997–2000   **Manager, Corporate Communications,** Blazing Entertainment, New York, NY

> Developed and communicated key corporate messages to multiple audiences, including customers, the media, investors, and employees.

> Coordinated publicity for launch of new Internet division; resulted in positive stories in dozens of major publications.

1995–1996   **Account Manager,** Jones & Pierce Public Relations, New York, NY

> Managed public relations for clients in the music industry, helping emerging artists increase exposure through extensive media outreach.

> Successfully handled communications crisis for high-profile client facing potentially negative publicity; coordinated interviews, drafted media statement, and handled press inquiries.

1994–1995   **Publicity Director,** Carrot Catering, Westport, CT

> Developed brochures, created advertisements, and coordinated media outreach for an event-catering business; publicity efforts increased business 50 percent in one year.

EDUCATION

B.A., Communications, Connecticut College

the functional résumé

A **functional résumé** organizes work experience under headings that correspond to your particular skills, not the jobs you had or how long you worked at them. For the increasing numbers of people who are changing jobs frequently—and switching careers almost as often—the chronological résumé, which lists the places you've worked by date, is not always the best format. The functional résumé has emerged as a better way to give coherence and focus to a career that is not easily or best described chronologically. This format is good if you want to change careers, because it highlights what you have done and are capable of doing, and de-emphasizes past job titles—which sometimes don't accurately reflect your skills.

A Section Headers

The titles of sections in a functional résumé are not set in stone, so feel free to experiment. Other options for the Experience section are Professional Experience, Relevant Experience, Skills and Accomplishments, or some combination of these, such as Skills and Experience. Employment History can also be called Work History or Work Experience. Just be sure the difference between the two sections is clear.

B Skills

Select two to three skills you have used in the past that are relevant to the job you want. These can be Graphic Design, Budget Management, Research, or even Basket Weaving, if that happens to be your line of work.

C Employment History

Even with a functional résumé, you still need to list the names of companies you have worked for, your job titles, and your dates of employment. That way, employers can still tell at a glance where you have worked—and for how long. But your accomplishments are described by organizing them into specific skills, which might otherwise get buried in a chronological format.

Chris West

310 Pacific Street, #4D, San Francisco, CA 94118
cwest@webmail.net   415-555-2464

A — SUMMARY OF QUALIFICATIONS

- Ten years' experience designing for print media, Web sites, and interactive products
- Thorough knowledge of computer technology and its impact on design requirements
- Skilled listener with the ability to assess and manage design needs of multiple departments

A — SKILLS & ACCOMPLISHMENTS

Interactive Product Development

- Created an expense report application purchased by more than 30 Fortune 500 companies.
- Developed navigation tools for Web site that won "Best of the Web" award.

Graphic Design

- Designed Web pages, corporate brochures, and annual report for major technology company.
- Streamlined production process for graphics creation at a deadline-oriented news site.
- Created award-winning print advertisements for beauty and fashion industry clients.

Collaboration & Management

- Managed design team, including photo editor, designers, and freelance photographers in fast-paced, demanding environment.
- Collaborated with marketing departments to determine business requirements, define technical limitations, and craft visual strategies.

A — EMPLOYMENT HISTORY

Director of User Experience Zeitgeist Software, Oakland, CA   2001–02
Freelance Designer Cambridge, MA   1999–00
Creative Director Compuquest Corp., Redmond, WA   1998–99
Design Director Dream Media, San Francisco, CA   1994–98

A — EDUCATION

Massachusetts Institute of Technology, MS, Media Technology
California Institute of the Arts, B.F.A., Graphic Design

the hybrid résumé

Traditional—
with a twist

For those on the fence between a chronological and a functional résumé, there is a way to have the best of both worlds. What is sometimes called a **hybrid résumé** is a combination of the two formats: the basic structure of a chronological résumé, with specific skills listed below each job description (see opposite page).

A hybrid résumé lets you draw more attention to your skills than you can with a purely chronological format, but it retains enough of the structure of a chronological résumé that it won't put off employers who don't like the functional format. In that sense, it is a safe bet for those who want to experiment.

With a hybrid résumé, you may want to include more detail in your **Summary of Qualifications** section (for more on this section, see page 36). By outlining specific skills at the top of your résumé, you can identify yourself right off the bat as a speech therapist, an art director, or a video editor—a profile that is reinforced in your Experience section by highlighting related skills.

But be careful to avoid too much repetition; try to list different but related skills below each job title. If you find yourself listing the same skill over and over, a functional résumé is probably a better option.

Kate Carpenter
2827 Elm Street, Vienna, VA 22180
kcarpenter@webmail.net 703-555-8974

OBJECTIVE: A position in the development or alumni office of a college or university.

SUMMARY OF QUALIFICATIONS

• Five years' experience working for nonprofit organizations, with an emphasis on fund-raising.

• Persuasive and articulate communicator with knowledge of educational organizations and their priorities.

• Energetic leader skilled at mobilizing and motivating volunteers.

EXPERIENCE

1999–present   **Program Manager,** Educational Reform Center, Vienna, VA

Fund-raising

• Developed brochure and coordinated mailing for a $1.5 million fund-raising campaign; managed 25 volunteers who participated in follow-up phone outreach to potential donors.

• Wrote grant application that secured a $500,000 award to fund experimental teacher training workshops.

Event Coordination

• Gained sponsorship for and organized a one-day workshop to educate teachers about using the Internet in the classroom.

1997–99   **Project Assistant,** Environmental Advocacy Foundation, Washington, D.C.

Grant Writing

• Assisted director in preparing proposals for grants from local and national foundations, helping generate $250,000 in funding.

• Completed a weeklong training seminar on nonprofit fund-raising and grant writing.

Research

• Reviewed studies on global warming; prepared a report on the effects of increased temperatures on coastal communities in developing countries.

EDUCATION

Georgetown University, B.A., History

what is a "CV"?

A CV is appropriate
for faculty or
overseas positions

Most professionals (doctors, lawyers, professors) forgo the typical résumé when looking for a job in favor of something called the **CV**, short for the Latin phrase *curriculum vitae* (which means "life's course"). A CV is much longer than a typical résumé (it can run five or more pages in length) and includes more detailed information about a candidate's publications, presentations, affiliations, and awards.

Who needs a CV?

A CV is most commonly used by academics applying for a faculty or research position; it is also used in the scientific community and by institutions devoted to research. Medical and legal professionals sometimes use a **professional résumé**, a shortened version of a CV in which education and professional training are usually listed above work experience, and job descriptions tend to be longer and more detailed. But if you do not have an advanced degree, chances are you do not need to worry about doing a CV—unless you are applying for a position abroad. In some countries outside the U.S., candidates are expected to submit an international CV (see details below) rather than a résumé.

What is an international CV?

An international CV is different from an academic CV in that sections such as Publications or Presentations are not necessarily expected (although anyone with published work or experience speaking at conferences would want to list those details). An international CV also frequently includes personal information such as age and marital status—details that are illegal for an employer to ask about in the U.S. but perfectly acceptable abroad. When applying for a job in a foreign country, it is best to research local practices before submitting a résumé or CV, since customs vary by country.

PAPERS DELIVERED

"Legislators and Bureaucrats: Barriers to Administrative
Reform," presented at the annual conference of the American
Political Science Association, Bos....

Sample Curriculum Vitae

Adam Rodgers
425 Elm Street, Ann Arbor, MI 54321
arodgers@webmail.net   734-555-2354

TEACHING EXPERIENCE

Professor of Political Science and Public Policy, University of
Michigan, 2000–present

Assistant Professor of Political Science, University of
California, Berkeley, 1996–2000

EDUCATION

Stanford University, Ph.D. in Political Science, 1996

Stanford University, M.A. in Political Science, 1992

Michigan State University, B.A. in Political Science, with
Departmental Honors, 1988

PUBLICATIONS

Election Reform and Development (Oxford University Press,
2002)

"Democracy and Election Reform," *Comparative Politics*,
April 2000, vol. 32, no. 3

GRANTS & FELLOWSHIPS

Visiting Research Fellow, Institute for Election Studies,
Buenos Aires, Argentina, 1995

Fulbright Grant for Doctoral Dissertation Research in Chile,
1993–94

résumé warm-up

Get the ideas flowing

Okay, you've got an ad for a job you are interested in. Great. Or perhaps you've heard about a job in your company that you think you'd like to apply for. Now you need to write a résumé that will get your foot in the door. How do you start? By comparing your experiences and accomplishments to the description of the job you are after:

■ If you are responding to a specific job opening, make a list of all the requirements the company gave for the position.

■ Then make a list of all the things you've done in previous positions that are related to those requirements. If you have limited or no previous work experience, use experience from volunteer work, school activities, or membership in an organization or club.

■ What awards or compliments have you received on the job or at school? Do any of them relate to the job you are seeking? Was your work ever recognized by your company or industry? Dig up past performance reviews (if you have them). If you don't, try to recall ways previous managers, colleagues, or customers complimented your work. Did you help cut costs, build a customer base, increase sales, or create efficiencies in work flow? Besides actual awards, even less-formal distinctions are worth noting.

FIRST PERSON SUCCESS STORY

Résumé Writer's Block

When I sat down to write my résumé, I got stuck almost immediately. I'd taken a year away from work to travel abroad, so I knew a functional format was probably best. But I'd never done one before and I kept second-guessing myself. Finally, I hit on the bright idea of asking everyone I knew to send me their résumés to use as samples. It was wonderful! I got some great ideas, and my friends and family members were flattered by the request. Several offered to check my résumé when I finished—and those extra sets of eyes helped, too!

Cheryl B., Pittsburgh, Pennsylvania

Overcoming a Blank Page

Looking at other résumés for guidance can help. Writing a résumé is not like taking an exam: It is okay to share your work. A former coworker or friend may have come up with a great way to describe something you have also done. You can also find sample résumés online at career sites or by plugging keywords into a search engine (e.g., "marketing manager" and "résumé"). But the idea is not to copy someone else's text wholesale, especially someone who is also on the job hunt. Use other ideas for inspiration, but make your résumé your own.

getting professional advice

Job hunting is tough on the psyche

Writing a résumé is not easy, but it can be especially difficult if you are unsure of what type of work you really want to do. If you are just starting out or want to make a career move, you need to know what career you want to get into before you can shape a résumé to target it. How do you know what kind of work is best for your skills and abilities?

First do some good old-fashioned soul searching. Ask yourself what you wanted to do when you were a child, a teenager, a young adult. Did you stick with your original job goals? What caused you to change your career path? What work options have you never dared to explore?

For help fleshing out those answers, consider consulting a professional. Career counselors analyze your job ambitions and match them up with real-life possibilities. How do they do this? One way is by having you take various tests for aptitudes and interests. Another way is to go through your job history and help you sort out those skills and talents you want to develop.

Once you are on track with the career that suits you and fires up your imagination, a career counselor can help you fine-tune a résumé that will help you attain it.

Hiring a Counselor

Think of a career counselor as a personal trainer, someone who is part expert, part coach. Fees for career counseling differ depending on where you live, but they run about the same as for marriage or personal counseling, usually anywhere from $50 to $100 an hour. Counselors sometimes offer group sessions that are reasonably priced. Such groups meet regularly to share ideas and experiences and to role-play interviews. If you have lost your job due to mass layoffs at your company, your outplacement benefits may include professional career counseling and even related support groups.

Here are some indicators of a qualified counselor:

■ The counselor charges by the hour (including a fee for the introductory interview).

■ There are no up-front payments or contracts committing you to a schedule of payments.

■ On the initial interview, you meet the counselor you'll be working with rather than a salesperson.

■ The counselor has a degree in social work or some other related field (see below).

Finding a Certified Counselor

National designations are either National Certified Counselor (NCC) or National Certified Career Counselor (NCCC). The latter is the more extensively skilled, with a graduate degree and supervised experience in the field of career counseling. State certifications differ; look for the departmental name on the certificate in the counselor's office, and check it out in the blue pages of your phone book that list your state government offices and departments.

To find certified career counselors in your area, call the National Board for Certified Counselors at 336-547-0607 (fax 336-547-0017) and request a list. Or send an e-mail through the group's Web site at **www.nbcc.org.**

now what do I do?

Answers to common questions

I work full-time, have two kids, and don't have enough time left over to do a thorough job updating my résumé. Can I hire someone to do it for me?

Yes, you can hire a freelance professional résumé writer. These are writers who have significant experience working on résumés. You can ask career counselors for referrals, check with friends or colleagues, or consult the yellow pages. Local employment agencies or industry associations may provide referrals as well. When you find a candidate, be sure to ask for references, and negotiate in advance how much it will cost—and how the writer will handle any revisions. Even if you hire professional help, you will probably have to do some revising on your own because no single résumé is adequate for every job you apply for.

I want to use a chronological format for my résumé, but my current job is not related to the field I want to work in. How can I de-emphasize my present position but still stick with the chronological style?

One option is to divide your work experience into two sections: Related (or Relevant) Experience and Other (or Additional) Experience. In the first section, list the positions that are most relevant to the job you want, then move the rest of your experience into a separate section below. Just be sure you list dates of employment clearly, so employers can tell when you were at each job.

I updated my résumé six months ago. Do I really need to revise it again to apply for a job opening I just saw?

Chances are there are a few things you'll want to change, even after just six months. Maybe your job objective should be changed to reflect the title of the position you are applying for, or you worked on a successful project in the past few months that you'll want to brag about. It's always a good idea to keep your résumé current.

I got a call from a recruiter about a job I'd like. Will the recruiter help me polish my résumé?

Most likely, no. A recruiter is a professional hired by a client company to fill certain designated job openings within that company. A recruiter's task is to identify and screen qualified candidates—not to help you, the potential candidate, get a job. So while a recruiter may make some suggestions on how you can improve your résumé before he passes it along to an employer, it will be up to you to revise it. And in most cases a recruiter will use whatever résumé you submit, so make sure you are happy with it before putting it in his or her hands.

Now where do I go?

CAREER COUNSELORS

National Career Development Association
www.ncda.org or **918-663-7060**

National Board for Certified Counselors
www.nbcc.org or **336-547-0607**

Five O'Clock Club
www.fiveoclockclub.com or **800-538-6645 ext. 600**

RESUME SERVICES

Professional Association of Résumé Writers & Career Coaches
www.parw.com or **800-822-7279**

National Résumé Writers' Association
www.nrwa.com or **888-679-2444**

BOOKS

What Color Is Your Parachute? 2003
by Richard Nelson Bolles

I Could Do Anything If I Only Knew What It Was: How to Discover What You Really Want and How to Get It
by Barbara Sher with Barbara Smith

Discover What You're Best At
by Linda Gale and Barry Gale

Getting started

Your résumé is not an outline for your biography; it is a sales tool.

the main sections

Describing what sections go into a résumé is a bit like describing what ingredients go into a spaghetti sauce: There are no hard and fast rules, but there are certain basic ingredients none should be without. Every résumé should include three main sections:

1. Contact information. Employers need to know how to reach you, so list your home address, a phone number (specify hours that you are reachable if you do not have an answering machine), and an e-mail address if you have one.

2. Summary of your work experience. No one is going to hire you without knowing where you have worked. There are also no set rules on what you should call this, or any, section on your résumé. But if you get too creative—say, calling your work experience "life lessons," employers may be turned off. Professional Experience, Work History, Work Experience, and Employment are all perfectly acceptable ways to describe your employment background.

3. Description of your educational background. Hiring managers want to know whether you dropped out of high school, have a college degree, or have done any graduate work.

Besides those three sections, many résumés include a **job objective**, a sentence or phrase describing what type of job you are looking for. It's become fairly common to include a **summary of qualifications**, either in addition to or instead of an objective. This section, sometimes called a **profile**, is a short, enthusiastic summary of your skills—the résumé equivalent to the teaser headlines on a magazine cover.

Note: Depending on your qualifications, there are a handful of other sections you might include as well, such as publications, affiliations, or awards, or a combination of the two (i.e., Affiliations & Awards). Keep in mind there is no one template that works for everyone. Pick and choose whatever fits your background and your goals.

Leigh Mitchum
1204 Panama Place, #4D, St. Albans, MO 12345
lmitchum@leemitchum.net   313-555-2464

SUMMARY OF EXPERIENCE

• Six years of office supervisory experience

• Managed and oversaw office relocation

• Handled accounting activities, including payroll, accounts payable, accounts receivable, and bookkeeping

EMPLOYMENT HISTORY

Office Supervisor, Morse Agency, St. Albans, MO 1997–present

• Manage real estate office, including bookkeeping and payroll, maintaining office supplies, and personnel records

• Supervise staff of five administrative assistants

• Assist in managing costs to meet budget requirements

• Work with IT team to implement new technology

Office Manager, Advantage Insurance, Savannah, MO 1993–1997

• Developed manual for business office procedures

• Filed insurance claims and handled applications

• Scheduled daily appointments and handled phone communications

• Worked with Web design company to launch Internet site

EDUCATION

Missouri Technical College, Savannah, MO (1991–1993). Related coursework: accounting, business communications, computer operations

contact information

Leigh Mitchum
1204 Panama Place #4D, St. Albans, MO 12345
lmitchum@leemitchum.net   313-555-2464

Putting your contact information—your name, address, and phone number—on your résumé is simple enough, but there are a few things to keep in mind. For starters, skip fancy designs and place your header at the top of the page, rather than at the bottom or sideways in the left margin. That way, it will be easier to convert your résumé to an e-mail–friendly format (see page 108 for more on e-mail conversion), where your name is easy to locate.

Name

If you have a gender-ambiguous name like Chris and want employers to know whether you'll show up for an interview in a tie or a skirt, list your full name (i.e., Christopher or Christine) or a middle name if that helps clarify your gender.

Address

If you plan to move shortly—say, you are graduating from college—include an address where you can be reached after you relocate. If a job listing indicates "local candidates only" and you are planning to move to the area, use a friend or relative's address so your application isn't tossed into the trash bin.

Phone Number

Besides your home phone, you may want to list a cell phone or work number—but only do so if you can answer those lines during business hours and it would not be awkward to talk about a new job. If you want to keep your search confidential, listing your work number may get you in hot water. You don't want to get a call about an interview while your boss is looking over your shoulder!

E-mail Address

These days, most employers expect to be able to reach applicants via e-mail. But some might be put off if you list your work e-mail address on your résumé, because it suggests you are conducting your search on company time. Use a personal address instead; you can get a free e-mail account from services like Yahoo or Hotmail. Also, your company may monitor employee e-mail, so corresponding about a job search at work could get you fired before you have found a new job.

Web Page

For some professions, it might make sense to include the address of your personal Web page on your résumé—if, for example, you are a graphic designer and have built a Web site with a portfolio of your work. But if your Web site also hosts your online diary and pictures of your seven cats, it may do more harm than good to share the address with prospective employers.

job objective

The pros and cons
of defining what
you want

Do you want to include an **objective**—a sentence or phrase describing the type of position you are looking for—on your résumé? Good question.

It depends. The benefit of listing an objective is that it tells an employer right off the bat what you want, e.g., "A position as a guidance counselor in a high school." The drawback is that some people have trouble describing their ideal position in a single sentence or prefer not to narrow the field. For instance, if you say your objective is "a position as an international rights manager for a publishing company," you might not be considered for an opening you would be perfectly happy with in another department.

If you have a very clear idea of the kind of position you want, an objective is probably a good idea—especially if you're specifically targeting a new field, industry, or position. But if you want to keep your options open, it would be better to leave the objective off and address your interests in your cover letter.

When to include an objective

- If you are responding to a classified ad or applying for a listed job opening, make the title of that position your objective.

- If you just graduated and/or have little work experience, list an objective that indicates what field you are interested in.

- If you want to change careers, including an objective will make it clear that you are pursuing a new path, rather than looking for a job in the same line of work.

- If your work history is diverse, use an objective to clarify what you want next, so employers don't have to guess.

Sample Objectives

"Administrative Assistant, Legal Affairs Division"

- Use the exact title of the position when replying to an ad for a job opening.

"Technology Training Manager"

- Keep it concise and clear if you are mass mailing companies and do not know whether they have any openings or what title they use for a particular job.

"A marketing position with a travel or recreation company"

- If you know you want to work in a particular industry, indicating that will give your objective some focus.

Tips

- Keep it short (a phrase is best; two or three sentences is overkill).

- Don't say you want an "entry level" position (you'll rule yourself out of consideration for other jobs).

- Make sure the rest of your résumé supports your objective (the accomplishments you highlight should demonstrate that you are qualified for the job you want).

summary of qualifications

You may want to include a summary of qualifications—sometimes referred to as a skills summary or a profile—section on your résumé. The goal of this brief listing is to highlight your strongest selling points relating to the job you want, so that employers quickly leafing through a pile of résumés can tell at a glance whether yours rates a second look. Think of it as a marketing brochure or an advertisement; the idea is to sell yourself.

You can use several sentences in a paragraph format, but since the point is to give a quick snapshot of your qualifications, bullet points may be preferable. Use statements that are targeted to your objective. If you're applying for a job as a sales representative, describing your "four years of experience as a paralegal for a law firm serving the banking industry" is less effective than saying you have "four years of experience satisfying client needs in banking and financial services."

What to include:

- **A phrase that gives an overview of your experience:**

"Eight years of experience as a technical writer for computer hardware and software manuals"

- **A summary of your credentials:**

"Certified public accountant with training in small business tax management"

- **An award or distinction you have received:**

"Honored as Media Planner of the Year by *Advertising Age* magazine in 2001"

- **A description of your skills:**

"Patient and understanding customer service representative able to calm angry callers"

What <u>Not</u> to Include

- **Bland phrases that lack specific details:**

"Good verbal and written communication skills."

- **Points that repeat verbatim a sentence you list elsewhere on your résumé**

Either find a way to reword the same idea or don't repeat it.

- **Long-winded sentences that are bogged down with jargon:**

"Detail-oriented, reliable, organized Systems Administrator with experience setting up, maintaining, and troubleshooting a wide variety of applications, including listservs, Oracle databases, and Web servers in both Windows and Unix environments."

A Summary or an Objective?

A summary or an objective gives a résumé a clear focus and helps hiring managers quickly get a handle on who you are and what you have to offer. But sometimes you may want to choose one or not include either. If you're trying to keep your résumé to one page, including both might take up more space than you can afford. And if you state clearly in your cover letter which job you are applying for, listing an objective on your résumé might be redundant. Similarly, some people find a summary knocks the wind out of their accomplishments. If, for example, you are just starting out, a summary will simply repeat the work experience listed below it. Choose whichever best fits your background. But keep in mind that if you opt against including either section, you will be automatically positioned by your most recent post.

your education

Make the most of your schooling

Whether you have been working for years or have never worked before, employers expect to find information on your résumé about your educational background. In most cases, all you need to list is the name of the college or university you attended and the degree you received; for example, Ohio State University, B.A., Political Science.

Recent college graduates often wonder which to list first: education or experience. Most people who have been out of school for more than a couple of years list their education at or near the bottom of their résumé. But if you just graduated from college—especially if you attended a prestigious school—you may want to list it higher, after your objective or summary. Or if you just received an advanced degree, such as an M.B.A., and are re-entering the workforce, it may improve your marketability to list your education early on. Also include your G.P.A. if it is impressive (3.4 or higher), and list any academic honors you received.

If you don't have a college degree and are applying for a job that requires a high school diploma, note on your résumé that you have one. Also include information about any college coursework you have completed, even if you did not get a degree, or any other training you have had, such as a vocational program.

List details about professional training related to your career under Education, which you can also call Education & Training or Education & Development. Examples include continuing education or certification courses in your field, such as a class to obtain a real estate license.

ASK THE EXPERTS

Should I list the date I graduated from college?

Only list the date you received your degree if you don't mind giving away your age. (By law, employers cannot ask how old you are in an interview.) In general, if more than 15 years have passed since you were in college, leave the date off. If you do include a graduation date, just list the year after your degree—no need to say it was May 30.

Should I include information about college activities or the thesis I wrote?

If you are a recent college graduate and have minimal work experience, you should definitely include details about activities you participated in, but limit yourself to organizations or affiliations that can help you get a job (it's best not to mention you organized your fraternity's annual Halloween beer bash). If you have no work experience, you may want to list activities such as writing for the school newspaper under Experience rather than Education. Describe your thesis if it relates to your job objective—if, say, you wrote about the evolution of political parties in the U.S. and are looking for a job on Capitol Hill. If you've been out of school for a while, focus on your professional accomplishments.

If I didn't go to college, can I skip the Education section on my résumé and wait for employers to ask about it?

No doubt famous college dropouts like Bill Gates don't highlight their education on a résumé, but unless you're the chairman of your own company—or similarly successful—it's likely the absence of information about your education will be noticed. Whether that leads an employer to toss your résumé or give you a call for clarification depends on who is doing the hiring or what the qualifications for the job are. It's okay to leave it out, but be honest when the question comes up in an interview. Include any college coursework or professional training classes under an Education section even if you did not complete a degree.

work experience

Describe your accomplishments

Many people find listing their work experience the most challenging part of writing a résumé. That's because it's hard to condense your job and your accomplishments into a few phrases. The first lesson to remember is that your résumé is not an outline for your biography; it is a marketing brochure, a sales tool to get you an interview or at least a phone call. So focus on presenting yourself as the ideal candidate for the job you want rather than getting bogged down by what you have done.

To get started, tackle the easy part first: Simply list the names of the companies you have worked for, your job title, and your dates of employment (list years, not months). It is also common practice to list where the company is located (city and state).

Next, describe your accomplishments at each job—what you achieved, not what you were responsible for. For example, saying you "exceeded sales goals by at least 10 percent every quarter" is much stronger than saying you "sold computer parts." You can use bullets or sentences in a paragraph format, but focus on three to five main accomplishments.

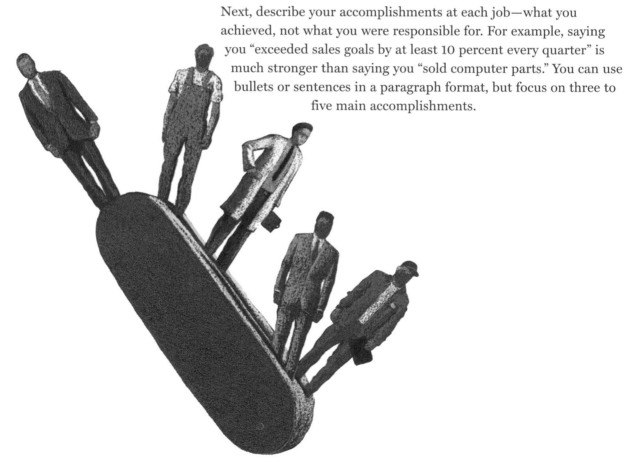

Tips for Describing Your Work Experience

■ **Focus on achievements that relate to your objective.**

You don't have to include everything you did on the job. Instead, focus on three to five accomplishments that relate to your career goal. Even if you only spent a third of your time managing training workshops, highlight that experience if you are applying for a job as director of training and development.

■ **Don't describe things you don't want to do.**

If you hated planning events and don't ever want to plan another one, don't bring it up on your résumé. Otherwise, employers will assume it is something you are still interested in doing.

■ **Keep your sentences short and simple.**

Remember, employers don't read every word on a résumé. Keep points short, and break up sentences that contain several clauses.

■ **Describe results, not just responsibilities.**

Structure accomplishments by describing a situation, the action you took or constraint you overcame, and then the result. This is where **action verbs** come in handy—verbs like "developed," "persuaded," "motivated," or "upgraded" that begin a sentence and dynamically capture what you have done (see page 60). But don't just say you "developed a marketing strategy" for a new brand of toothpaste. Let prospective employers know it resulted in your company's most successful product launch ever in the youth market.

optional sections

There are a handful of other sections, such as professional organizations you belong to or awards you have won, that you might want to include on your résumé, depending on your background. Focus on things that are relevant to your career goals; if you list every organization you've ever participated in, you risk diluting your résumé's focus. If you're already short on space, try to combine two sections, such as Affiliations & Awards, so your résumé doesn't feel cluttered. Some options to consider include:

Affiliations & Organizations

Employers like to hire people who are active in their industry or community because this demonstrates teamwork and networking skills. So if you are a member of any organizations, serve as a director on any boards, or otherwise participate in any groups, include it. This is also a good place to list any licenses or certifications you have received, such as Licensed Marriage & Family Child Counselor.

Honors & Awards

Another optional section, if you have received any distinctions, is Honors and Awards (which can also be called Distinctions, or whatever seems appropriate). You don't need to have won a Nobel Prize or a Pulitzer to include this section, but you also don't want to overplay something small. Being chosen Employee of the Month is better cited as part of your work history, rather than in a separate Awards section. Also, if you only have one award to list, it may be best to include it in another section.

Publications & Presentations

Listing books or papers you have written shows that you are respected in your field, but unless you are an academic, keep the citations short. If you are applying for a job that requires public speaking, include any major presentations you have given that illustrate your public speaking skills. If you are often asked to participate in conferences as a speaker, choose a couple of examples to highlight your experience or just summarize.

Sample Résumé Sections

Affiliations & Organizations

- Computer Press Association, Vice President 1997–1999, New York

- New Media Association, 1999–present, New York

Honors & Awards

- National Magazine Award, 1997, feature article on famine in Africa nominated

- *Best American Essays*, 1994, column on school choice selected for inclusion

Publications & Presentations

- "Educational Barriers to Development," published in *Latin America Quarterly* journal, 1999

- Keynote speaker, various conferences on political and economic development, including the Latin America International Development Forum, 2000

listing volunteer work

**Good works
are a plus**

Volunteer work is a great way to round out your résumé. There are several ways to include charity work on your résumé—the project or projects you should choose depends on the other experience you have and the type of job you are looking for. It's also important not to make it seem as though you were a paid employee, which would be a misrepresentation prospective employers could easily discover.

If you were an unpaid intern . . .

It's okay to list your title, the name of the organization or company, and your accomplishments with the rest of your work experience, but call the section Experience or Work History rather than Employment (which suggests you were an employee). If you indicate you were an intern, prospective employers won't be surprised if they call up the company and find out there's no record of your employment.

If you volunteered while taking time off . . .

Again, you can still list your volunteer work under Experience or a similar title, but if you volunteered for an organization that has nothing to do with your career path, you're probably better off putting it in a separate category, such as Other Experience. Or, if you use a functional résumé (see page 16), just list your volunteer position under Work History to indicate what you were doing during an employment gap.

If your volunteer work is extracurricular . . .

If you volunteer at the local children's hospital on weekends or evenings off and want prospective employers to know about it, list it in a category such as Affiliations and Community Service.

Using Volunteer Work to Open Doors

If you're between jobs or trying to change careers, doing volunteer work is a good way to add new skills to your portfolio or show that you were doing something productive during a period of unemployment. Here's how and where to get started.

■ **Get involved in an industry or professional association.**

Most industries have trade associations that use volunteers to organize meetings, staff events, or help out with mailings and other tasks. This is a good way to network if you are new to a particular career or have relocated to a new city. To find the right group, call your local Chamber of Commerce, consult the *Encyclopedia of Associations* at your local library, or search online for the name of your industry and city—e.g.,"advertising/association/Chicago."

■ **Donate your time in the community.**

If there's no local trade association in your community, volunteering with an organization unrelated to your field can still help you make contacts and fill in a gap in your résumé—not to mention provide more altruistic rewards. Go online and check sites like **www.volunteermatch.org** (it can match you with opportunities in the area), check for volunteer opportunities columns in local newspapers, or look in your phone book for local resources.

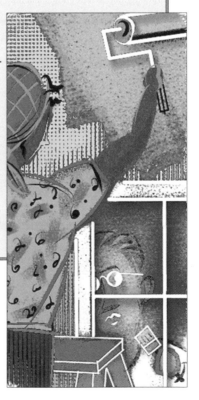

what to leave out

When writing a résumé, less is often more—and there are some details it is best to leave out altogether.

Don't get personal

Although personal information is sometimes found on résumés in other countries—such as a date of birth, marital status, health condition, or information about any children—in the U.S. these details would not be considered appropriate. Also, unless your hobbies and personal interests are directly relevant to the job you want, don't include them. If you are an avid basketball player applying for a staff position with the NBA, find a subtle way to work in your passion; for instance, you can note that you played basketball in college in your Summary of Qualifications or Education section.

If it goes without saying, don't bother saying it

There is no need to say "References available upon request" or "Portfolio available for review." Employers already know that and would not hesitate to ask. Cluttering up your résumé with such extraneous information can distract from your qualifications—or worse, make you seem inexperienced.

Avoid talking about salary

Although many classified ads ask applicants to respond with their salary requirements, a résumé is not the place to raise this topic. You can discuss the issue more deftly in your cover letter (see page 136), but if possible it's best to wait until an interview to discuss compensation—and then let the employer bring it up.

ASK THE EXPERTS

I'm applying for a position with a cancer support group, and I am a cancer survivor. Shouldn't I mention that I've had the disease?

If you are applying for a job and some aspect of your personal life is relevant to the position—as in this case—it's appropriate and probably useful to include that information. Making note of it in your Summary of Qualifications is one option, or you could include a section called Other Related Experience. Finally, you could mention and describe your experience in your cover letter. But be careful not to divulge too many details about a medical condition; some employers may be wary of candidates with serious health problems.

I'm active in a national religious movement and have won several honors for my work. Should I include them on my résumé?

In most cases, it's best not to reference memberships in religious or political organizations, or groups that might reveal other personal information, such as your race or sexual orientation. The unfortunate reality is that employers may not be as objective as they should be when considering you for a job. (An exception would be when information is relevant to your career—if, for example, you are applying for a position as a legislative assistant, it is okay to reveal your political affiliation.) When in doubt, leave it out.

FIRST PERSON DISASTER STORY

Priced Out

A friend sent me a job listing for an opening in his company's quality assurance department. The ad said, "Please indicate salary requirements," so in my objective I wrote that I was looking for a position as a quality assurance tester that paid $60,000. I didn't get an interview, and my friend told me later he heard about my résumé at a department meeting. It turns out they pay Q.A. testers $45,000. Now I wish I had left that figure out!

Benjamin B., Augusta, Maine

using computer templates

Think of them as résumé cheat sheets

Now that you have thought through what sections you want on your résumé and have a rough idea of how to describe your job accomplishments, you can simply start typing it up on your home computer. If you have Microsoft Word software, you are in luck. Most versions of Microsoft Word—by far the most common word processing program—include a Résumé Wizard that will walk you through the process of creating a résumé template and filling it in with your own information. (See opposite page for directions.)

If you don't have Microsoft Word, there are a number of résumé-creation software programs you can buy, most available for under $40. To find out more about these programs, ask a local retailer or visit the software section at **www.cnet.com**. Enter "resume" in the search field to find product reviews and software downloads.

RED FLAG

If you use a software program to create your résumé, be careful about relying too much on the standard template. Change the font slightly or make some other alteration so yours will stand out.

STEP BY STEP

Using Résumé Templates in Microsoft Word

Here's how to access the Résumé Wizard on a computer running Windows. (On a Macintosh, open a new document and you should see similar choices.)

1. Click on the Start Menu.

2. Choose New Office Document.

3. Click on the tab that says Other Documents.

4. Choose Résumé Wizard.

The Résumé Wizard will then walk you through a series of questions, such as what résumé format you want to use (chronological vs. functional) and what sections you would like to include (Objective, Summary of Qualifications, Education, etc.). It will create a document with appropriate headers and directions about what needs to be filled in, such as job titles, details about your position, and dates of employment.

You can then save the document to your hard drive and revise it later as you would any other Microsoft Word file.

now what do I do?

Answers to common questions

Two of the companies I worked for in the past five years are no longer in business. Do I have to indicate that on my résumé?

It's probably best not to raise the issue directly. Your aim is to land an interview, so why risk turning off a prospective employer with the taint of your former company's failure? But if the need to explain why your job tenures were short outweighs that concern, there are clues you can give that will get the point across. For example, somewhere in your description of the position, clarify that the company was "an Internet startup building technology to link companies with suppliers" or that it "moved to North Dakota after a merger."

Do I have to list every job I have ever had? How far back do I go?

If you have been working for more than 10 years, it's okay to focus on your most recent work experience and leave out ancient history. The actual number of jobs you list depends on how frequently you have moved around; someone with three jobs in 15 years should list them all, but if you had eight jobs in that time period you may want to leave one or two out. Even if you have been working less than 10 years, there may be a position or two after college it makes sense to skip. But don't leave yourself with any awkward gaps in the middle of your career; consider using a functional résumé if you prefer to downplay a recent job.

What if I did work my boss took credit for? Can I list it?

Yes, as long as you do not overstate your contributions. And if you work in a community or industry where gossip gets around, be careful how you phrase things—you don't want to divulge something unflattering about a former boss. For example, if you wrote all of your boss's speeches but she took credit for them, it is more tactful to say on your résumé that you "drafted speeches for upper-level executives" than to specify who you are talking about.

I've held several job titles at the same company. How should I list the different positions on my résumé?

You can list each position separately (with selected accomplishments below each title) or list all your titles and then highlight several accomplishments that capture your time with the company. In some cases, it's okay to list your most recent title and then note in your job description that you were promoted—e.g., "promoted from executive assistant after three months."

Now where do I go?

WEB SITES

www.volunteermatch.org
Helps those interested in volunteer work find organizations in their community.

www.cnet.com
A resource for résumé software; search under "resume" to find product reviews and software downloads.

www.jobstar.org
A free site offering résumé writing tips, as well as sample chronological and functional résumés.

BOOKS

Résumé Catalog: 200 Damn Good Examples
by Yana Parker

Franklin Covey Style Guide for Business and Technical Communication
by Franklin Covey

Make a Difference: Your Guide to Volunteering and Community Service
by Arthur I. Blaustein

Your first draft

Your first draft got
the basic points down on paper;
now you'll focus on the details
that will make your résumé stand out.

a second look

Great! You've filled in the main sections of your résumé. Now it's time to go back through your document and polish it up. Your first draft got the basic points down on paper; now you'll focus on the details that will make your résumé stand out.

If you're writing your résumé in one sitting, take a break before you give it a second shot. With fresh eyes, you will notice things you can improve or clarify that you might otherwise miss.

When you are ready to take another pass, here are a few questions you should ask yourself.

Résumé Checklist

1. Is your résumé easy to read?
Read through your résumé and mark wherever you stumble on a phrase or find a sentence that goes on and on. (Better yet, close the door and read your résumé out loud.) If you find that reading your résumé is like trudging through mud, everyone else will too. Make sure your résumé is easy to read—or it won't get read at all.

2. Is it brief and to the point?
A typical manager spends between 10 seconds and a few minutes reading a résumé, which means you need to keep your reader's attention span in mind as you write and revise your document. Unless you have a decade of experience, try to keep it to one page. But if confining yourself to one page means tiny type and narrow margins, a two-page résumé is preferable. A résumé that is easy to scan is more likely to be read than one that crams as much information as possible on the page, forcing the reader to figure out which points are most relevant.

3. Does your résumé support your objective?
Your accomplishments should target your objective—or the job you are applying for, if you didn't include an objective. If, for example, you have said you want to manage a retail store, your résumé should include experience in sales or supervising others.

4. Does your personality come across?

Even though your résumé should not include personal information, you do want to convey some aspect of your personality in your résumé, particularly as it relates to work. If you are reliable, get along well with others, or always pitch in when your colleagues are overworked, those traits should come across in your Summary or somewhere in your work experience.

5. Is your résumé engaging?

Make sure your résumé has something interesting to grab onto. If you think your résumé is boring, you can bet that the person you send it to will, too. Faced with hundreds or even thousands of résumés from people who might all be qualified for a particular job, employers will pick a handful of applicants to interview based on which résumés grab their interest.

6. Are you being honest?

Your résumé should highlight your accomplishments—this is no time for modesty. But if patting yourself on the back turns into exaggeration or outright lies, you are setting yourself up for trouble.

7. Is it easy to understand?

Résumés are frequently copied, forwarded, and passed around the office, so yours may end up on the desk of someone other than the original recipient. Since you have no idea how far afield yours will travel, avoid using department-specific jargon that won't make sense to other managers.

8. Is it computer-friendly?

Some companies use computers to scan résumés into a database that can later be searched by any hiring manager within the company (see page 114). Try to find out how the companies you are contacting review résumés so you can draft yours to fit their recruiting processes.

9. Will you be able to validate your résumé verbally?

Employers and recruiters will ask you questions about the information on your résumé. Know your résumé well enough that you can support its claims under a pressure situation such as a job interview.

demonstrating results

Showcase your accomplishments

Now you're ready to look at your accomplishments. Are you just listing what you did at each job or, much more effectively, describing the results your work brought about?

For example, a therapist could summarize her daily duties as "talking to patients all day," but that's simplistic—and uninspiring—as compared to saying that she "helped patients resolve anxiety disorders" or "recommended strategies for coping with loss."

Even if you think your work experience is too vague to quantify— after all, not all of us can say we "increased sales 35 percent in three months"—there are still many ways you can demonstrate specific results.

- **Say how long it took to do something.**
  "Completed project to convert company to new e-mail software two months ahead of six-month schedule"

  "Gathered financial data requested by clients consistently ahead of 24-hour turnaround time"

- **Indicate the scope of a project.**
  "Managed $125,000 advertising budget"

  "Trained 170 employees to use new software"

- **Highlight a particular achievement.**
  "Won a contract for a major catalog company"

  "Recommended photographer chosen for high-profile campaign"

- **Talk about a change.**
  "Reduced employee turnover by implementing flextime"

  "Implemented new ordering process that decreased delivery time for equipment by 50 percent"

- **Discuss the response to your work.**
  "Researched and implemented new technology that improved productivity by 15 percent"

  "Developed multimedia presentation that generated more than 200 leads from one conference"

HAT IF

I'm an assistant and all I do is answer phones, sort through the mail, and file documents. I don't have any accomplishments!

Sure you do—you just need to take a different approach to thinking about your work. Maybe you've managed multiple phone lines in a busy environment, and have become skilled at prioritizing and routing callers. Or you developed a new or more efficient filing system for your boss. Think about a time when someone complimented you on your work, or you felt good about how you handled a problem—whatever you come up with is most likely an accomplishment.

I'm a teacher and have nothing to do with sales or revenue or budgets! How can I quantify my accomplishments?

Results don't have to be demonstrated with numbers, and they don't have to involve company profits. Certainly in a classroom you have contributed to a lot of accomplishments—helping children overcome learning difficulties, develop problem-solving skills, work in teams, etc. Think about what your efforts produced and talk about those results.

I handle many different tasks—citing just three or four accomplishments doesn't seem like a complete picture of my work.

Don't worry about covering everything you do on the job—focus on the skills that relate to your objective, and make sure whatever you mention creates a coherent profile of your abilities (i.e., the things you cite are not four isolated accomplishments that don't seem to have anything to do with one another). The point is to get an interview, where you'll have time to talk about your other skills.

eliminating
wordy language

**Keep it simple
and focused**

The secret to good writing is knowing what to leave out. That rule applies to résumés. With a résumé, it is extremely important to keep things concise and focused. Remember, employers spend between 10 seconds and a few minutes reading each résumé, so make sure yours is easy to scan by following these tips to keep it short.

■ **Avoid being redundant.**
If you've repeated the same point over and over—e.g., that you have managed computer crises at several jobs—choose something else to highlight for one of the positions (for instance, that you consistently completed projects before your deadlines).

■ **Don't try to explain everything you've done.**
Even though most people do more than three or four things at every job, that's as much as you should talk about because people reading your résumé can't absorb a whole lot more. Highlighting several accomplishments well is more effective than risking information overload by listing six to eight bullet points below each job.

■ **Cut out unnecessary phrases and words.**
You don't have to write in complete sentences on a résumé. Leave out the pronoun "I," skip "a," "an," and "the," and avoid unnecessary phrases like "responsible for." (Just say "wrote employee newsletter" rather than "responsible for writing the employee newsletter for the company.")

Bullets vs. Text Descriptions

Another way to make your résumé more readable is to use bullet points rather than a paragraph of text to describe your accomplishments at each job. Although using bullets may take up more space than cramming a few phrases together in a paragraph, it will be much easier to scan—see the difference below.

Text

English Teacher, International Language Institute
Santiago, Chile
1998–2000

Taught English as a Second Language (E.S.L.) in group and private lessons to executives aged 25–65. Created curriculum and taught course on preparing applications for U.S. graduate schools, resulting in a 75% acceptance rate among students who submitted applications after completing the course. Developed supplemental teaching and testing materials to engage students, using English-language periodicals, tapes of television programs, and comic books.

Bullets

English Teacher, International Language Institute
Santiago, Chile
1998–2000

- Taught English as a Second Language (E.S.L.) in group and private lessons to executives aged 25–65.

- Created curriculum and taught course on preparing applications for U.S. graduate schools, resulting in a 75% acceptance rate among students who applied to schools after completing the course.

- Developed supplemental teaching and testing materials to engage students, using English-language periodicals, tapes of television programs, and comic books.

using action verbs

You've probably heard that you should use action verbs on your résumé, but many people would be hard pressed to define what they are. An action verb, sometimes called an active verb, is a verb that expresses an action, like "created," "developed," or "resolved."

On a résumé, action verbs are considered preferable to "being" verbs, such as "am," "is," "are," "was," or "were," because they allow you to avoid using passive voice. (Passive voice is when a sentence uses a verb followed by a past participle, like "He was nominated" or "Designs were chosen.") Action verbs ensure that you are the subject and focus of your résumé. They also make the text more dynamic and easier to read than it would be in passive voice.

formulated

motivated

maintained

facilitated

created

assessed

Action Doesn't Mean Sports

Don't feel you have to come up with off-the-wall action verbs, like "cajoled" or "multitasked"—it's okay to stick with the ones you find in most résumé books. Getting too creative may put off your reader, so use language that sounds natural. Also, don't confuse action verbs with sports metaphors. Using verbs like "punted," "kicked," "nailed," "swept," or "drilled" is a bit too casual—not to mention aggressive.

Sample Action Verbs

acted	identified	presented	addressed	implemented
produced	advised	improved	promoted	analyzed
increased	proposed	assessed	initiated	ran
briefed	installed	recommended	built	integrated
recruited	clarified	introduced	reduced	conceived
investigated	represented	coordinated	launched	researched
created	led	resolved	designed	lowered
restructured	determined	maintained	revamped	devised
managed	secured	developed	marketed	selected
directed	monitored	shaped	documented	motivated
shepherded	edited	negotiated	sold	enforced
opened	solved	established	organized	started
evaluated	outlined	streamlined	examined	oversaw
supervised	facilitated	performed	taught	formulated
planned	trained	headed	prepared	wrote

maintaining consistency

Don't switch styles
midway through

No matter which résumé style you've chosen, it's important to maintain consistency in formatting and punctuation. That way, employers know what to expect as they read through your résumé. (Keeping things consistent also demonstrates attention to detail—an important trait for any job.)

Run through this checklist to make sure you're sticking with the same style.

Format

■ If you use bullet points for one job description, don't switch to a text paragraph for the others.

■ List your title, company name, location, and dates of employment in the same order for each job.

Punctuation

■ If you use a period at the end of your first bullet point, use one for other bullets throughout your document. (Or, if you leave out the period on one, keep it off on the rest.)

■ If you use a comma before the word "and" in one list—known as a serial comma—stick with that style for other lists joined by "and" or "or."

■ If you capitalize your job title once, do the same with your other jobs.

Typeface

■ Don't change the font, or typeface, from one line to the next. It's okay to change the size to distinguish certain blocks of text, like the section headers or your contact information, but it's usually best to stick with one font style.

■ If you capitalize the letters in one header, like OBJECTIVE, do the same for the others.

ASK THE EXPERTS

What tense should I use if I'm still at my current job?

One exception to the consistency rule comes when choosing which tense to use when describing your work experience. Use the past tense for former jobs (e.g., "installed equipment") and the present tense for your current position (e.g., "negotiate contracts"), unless you're describing a project you finished at your present job, in which case use the past tense for that accomplishment.

Do I have to include the location of all of my employers?

Though not a hard and fast rule, it's generally a good idea to list the city and state (but not the street address) of your employers. Note: If you list a city and state for one position, be sure to do it for the rest; otherwise, it will look like you forgot to include it.

Do I have to use the same number of bullet points for each job?

Definitely not. You should devote more space to recent positions and less to earlier jobs. Your current position may warrant four or five bullet points or sentences whereas others might require just two or three, and a job you had long ago may have just one brief summary.

Sample Good Résumé

Christine Green
280 Fresno Street, #4D, Albion, MI 12345
cgreen@webmail.net   313-555-2464

OBJECTIVE

To obtain a Senior Level Paralegal position that enables me to utilize my skills and offers opportunity for professional development.

SUMMARY OF QUALIFICATIONS

- Five years' legal experience in medical malpractice and personal injury litigation
- Skilled in preparing legal documents quickly and accurately under deadline pressure
- Strong computer skills, including proficiency in Internet research and knowledge of Microsoft Word, Excel, and PageMaker software programs
- NALA certified

WORK EXPERIENCE

1997–present **Litigation Paralegal,**
Pearson, Coleman & Gillet, Albion, MI

- Prepare legal documents, client correspondence, settlement brochures, and related correspondence
- Interview clients, experts, witnesses to collect trial-related information
- Gather and interpret medical records, research cases, and provide written summaries for attorneys
- Provided documentation and legal research for five successful personal injury cases in which damages totaled between $12M and $25M

EDUCATION/CERTIFICATION

NALA Certified Legal Assistant, 1997

Certificate, Michigan State University Paralegal Program, 1997

Certificate, Litigation and Trial Practice, Michigan State University, Paralegal Program, 1998

Courses in Internet Research, Michigan State University, 1999

PROFESSIONAL AFFILIATIONS

2000–present Michigan Paralegal Association

2001–present Michigan Bar Association

Layout offers plenty of white space, minimal font changes, and effective use of bullet points, which make it easier to read and more visually inviting.

1. Contact information includes both a phone number and an e-mail address and clearly defines gender.

2. Objective is concise and references the title of the job advertised.

3. Summary highlights strongest selling points in an easy-to-read bullet format.

4. Detailed descriptions of specific accomplishments, use of action verbs, and bullet format strengthen presentation.

5. Education section includes degrees received and appropriate additional training.

Christine Green
280 Fresno Street, #4D, Albion, MI 12345
313-555-2464

OBJECTIVE

Seeking a paralegal position at a top law firm that cares about its clients and will allow me to utilize my vast knowledge and experience in customer relations, while also challenging me to increase my skills in order to best serve all of the clients.

SUMMARY OF QUALIFICATIONS

Skilled, NALA-certified paralegal with five years' legal experience in medical malpractice and personal injury litigation; a proficiency preparing legal documents quickly and accurately under deadline pressure; and strong computer skills, including expertise in Internet research.

WORK EXPERIENCE

1997–present Litigation Paralegal, Pearson, Coleman & Gillet, Albion, MI

• Responsibilities include preparing legal documents, client correspondence, settlement brochures, and related correspondence, as well as interviewing clients, experts, and witnesses to collect trial-related information.

• Work with attorneys, researching cases, gathering and interpreting medical records, providing written summaries for attorneys, organizing documents for trial, and assisting with jury instructions.

EDUCATION

Certificate, Michigan State University Paralegal Program, 1997

Certificate, Litigation and Trial Practice, Michigan State University, Paralegal Program, 1998

Overly verbose descriptions, use of multiple fonts, and lack of action verbs all contribute to this résumé's ineffectiveness.

1. Include an e-mail address as well as a phone number to give potential employers a choice of contact points.

2. Too long—a phrase or single sentence is best.

3. Summaries that pack too much information into one unwieldy sentence will alienate hiring managers.

4. Long-winded sentences in passive voice are dull and difficult to read.

5. Don't omit any extra training and professional affiliations that may help your résumé stand out.

more writing tips

Follow the rules of good grammar and writing

Remember diagramming a sentence in English class? Well, when writing a résumé, the basic rules you learned in high school or college English classes still apply. If you're rusty on grammar and writing rules, brush up with a writing guide like *The Elements of Style*, by William Strunk Jr. and E.B. White. Here are a few more résumé-specific writing tips to keep in mind.

■ **Break up long sentences.**
If your sentences are running past three lines on the page, break them into separate ideas—or eliminate unnecessary phrases.

■ **Keep it natural.**
Don't use words on a résumé you wouldn't use in a conversation. "Reduced departmental spending" is better than "actualized a plan to reduce departmental spending."

■ **Avoid overused phrases.**
Certain phrases have become so overused on résumés that they've lost any real meaning. Find other ways to say you are "detail oriented," a "self-starter," or have "excellent communication skills."

■ **Don't be vague.**
Give specific details about your work experience that will grab your reader's attention, and clarify any points that aren't obvious. For example, clarify that an employer named Davis & Sons is a restaurant supplier. Using vague or generic descriptions will guarantee that your résumé gets lost in the shuffle.

■ **Prioritize.**
When describing your work experience, start with your most impressive accomplishment at each position, even if it's something you did your first month on the job. Employers may only read the first line or two below your job titles, so don't let your best points be overlooked.

Get a Second Opinion

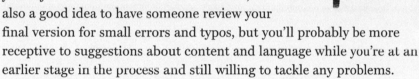

Once you think your résumé is in good shape—but before you consider it done—show it to a friend or colleague and ask for feedback. It's often better to solicit opinions midway through the process than to wait until you're just about to send it out. Of course, it's also a good idea to have someone review your final version for small errors and typos, but you'll probably be more receptive to suggestions about content and language while you're at an earlier stage in the process and still willing to tackle any problems.

FIRST PERSON DISASTER STORY

Trying Too Hard

The last time I updated my résumé, I decided to make myself sound more well-read. So I used a lot of fancy words I found in a thesaurus, like "envisaged" and "propagated" and a few others I had never used in my life. Fortunately, I showed my résumé to my wife before I sent it out. She highlighted all the words that sounded phony and asked me to define them and, of course, I couldn't. I realized that if she had been an interviewer I would have sunk my chances for getting a job. I revised that version and came up with descriptions that sounded a lot more natural.

Dave S., Portland, Oregon

the one-page dilemma

Sometimes a longer
résumé is appropriate

A hotly debated topic among career advisors is whether or not résumés should be limited to one page. Back in the days when résumés were usually sent through the mail or by fax, there was a stronger argument for fitting everything onto a single 8-1/2" x 11" piece of paper. But with more and more people applying for jobs online, the single-page mind-set has given way to more flexibility on length.

For one thing, when an e-mail message is printed, it includes additional information (like the "to," "from," and "date" fields), so even if you e-mail a one-page résumé, it will probably be longer once the recipient prints the document.

You should still, however, try to keep your résumé to one page, particularly if you are just out of college or have had only two or three jobs. Since résumé readers are often time-pressed, one page is always preferable if you can effectively express your qualifications in that amount of space.

But if you've been working for more than 10 years or have held many diverse positions during your career, limiting yourself to a single page may not do justice to your skills and experience. In that case, don't short-change yourself—add another page. Employers may say they prefer receiving one-page résumés, but if two pages means you include more white space and clearer descriptions, your document will ultimately be easier to read.

ASK THE EXPERTS

I only have five years of work experience, but I can't seem to get my résumé down to a single page. Is it all right if just a few lines appear on the second page?

Try putting your contact information (address, phone number, and e-mail address) on one line or going through your text and trimming a few words here and there that might save you a line. If that doesn't work, see page 106 for more space-saving hints.

I definitely need a two-page résumé. Should I repeat my contact information on the second page?

No, but you do need to include your name and page number at the top of the second page (and any subsequent pages). Also, avoid running sentences from one page to the next. If possible, don't start a job description on one page and continue it on the next. Finish with a position on the first page, then start the next page with a new job or section. And try to hit the highlights on the first page; you don't want to lose your audience before they get to the best points. Finally, if you're doing a CV, put "continued" on the bottom of the first page (and any other pages before the last one).

spelling and grammar

When it comes to
proofreading, you
can't be too careful

This part is simple—but very important. Since your résumé reflects your work ethic as well as your accomplishments, you want it to be absolutely perfect, which means it's essential to proofread every word before sending it out. Follow these steps to prevent any spelling or grammar mistakes from slipping through.

1. Double-check your digits.
Of course you know your address and phone number, and there's only a 1 in 1,000 chance you would have typed it wrong. Double-check it anyway—you don't want to miss out on an interview because the last digit in your phone number was wrong.

2. Eliminate spelling and grammar mistakes.
Now that Microsoft Word and other word processing programs can automatically check for spelling and grammar errors, there's no excuse for mistakes or typos. Take advantage of the spell-check feature when you finish your résumé and every time you revise it before sending it out.

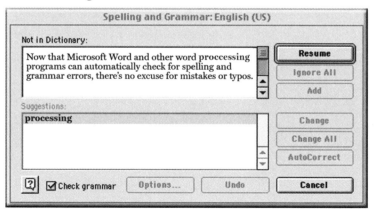

3. Give it a final proofread.
Don't just rely on the computer to find spelling and grammar mistakes—your computer won't know if you misspelled the name of a company you used to work for, and it isn't 100 percent foolproof when it comes to finding spelling or grammar problems. Read your résumé carefully and be on the lookout for errors the computer might not have caught. When you're satisfied, ask a friend to read it as well. A fresh pair of eyes may spot something you've overlooked.

ASK THE EXPERTS

Do I call to check that my résumé was received?

If an employer indicates in a classified ad how the company prefers to receive résumés, don't buck the system. This isn't the time to show your initiative by digging up the hiring manager's e-mail address when a company has asked candidates to reply to a fax number. If a friend at the company, however, suggests you contact the person doing the screening and gives you an e-mail address or phone number, by all means take the direct route—but be sure to mention right off the bat that so-and-so said you should get in touch.

Many job listings specifically say "No phone calls." Whether to follow this directive is a tougher decision. Since most people find the phone more intrusive than e-mail, you're probably better off sending an e-mail message to request more details about a position, find out if a decision has been made, or ask some other question besides "Did you get my résumé?" (an inquiry employers generally find irritating). If possible, contact an assistant to the hiring manager—someone lower in the office hierarchy may have more patience for questions than the person making the final hiring decisions.

now what do I do?

Answers to common questions

What if one of my main accomplishments was a group effort? How do I avoid taking credit for the whole project myself?

Start your sentence by acknowledging you were part of a team; for instance, "Member of team that re-engineered company billing system, reducing operating expenses by more than 10 percent a year."

What if I don't have a computer—is it okay to send a handwritten résumé if I write neatly?

It's pretty unlikely you'll be called for an interview if you submit a handwritten résumé for a job. If you don't have a computer but know how to use one, go to your local library or a business that rents computer time. (Take a disk so you can save a copy of your résumé for later revision.) If you don't know how to use a computer, look in your phone book under "résumé" or "word processing" to find someone you can hire to type your résumé for you.

Where do I find the bullet symbol on my computer?

In Microsoft Word, first type or highlight the text you want to appear after the bullet. Then click the Format menu and select Bullets and Numbering. A new window will open that will allow you to select which style of bullet you want to use. Select the image you like and then click the OK button. (If you are e-mailing your résumé, you may lose some format features like bullets. For more information about formatting a résumé for e-mail use, see page 108.)

My résumé is three pages. Is that too long?

Unless you are doing a CV, are a high-level executive, or have been working more than 20 years, three pages is most likely a page too long. If you can't find places to trim on your own, get a friend to help you, or consider hiring someone to review your efforts.

Does every sentence in my résumé have to begin with an action verb?

Not necessarily. Most sentences probably will start with an action verb (a verb that expresses actions you've taken such as "created" or "developed"; for more action verbs, see page 61). However, another alternative might be something like, "Chosen out of 40 trainees for promotion to a management position."

Now where do I go?

WEB SITES

Finding Action Verbs Online

www.rockportinstitute.com
At this career counseling company's site, click on How to Write a Masterpiece of a Résumé and then on the button Power Verbs.

Do a search for the phrase "action verbs" at a search site like Google (**www.google.com**) or Yahoo (**www.yahoo.com**) and you'll find lists of hundreds of action verbs posted online by schools, college career centers, and employment Web sites.

BOOKS

Writing Style Guides

The Elements of Style
by William Strunk Jr. and E.B. White

The New York Times Manual of Style and Usage
by Allan M. Siegal and William G. Connolly

The Chicago Manual of Style
by John Grossman (Editor)

Overcoming challenges

After running your own business
you may run into
certain negative perceptions
back in the job market.

minimizing résumé problems

Put a positive spin on your experience

Just about anyone sitting down to write a résumé has some gap, setback, or detour along their career path they want to de-emphasize as they go out on the job market.

Whether you've been a full-time parent for five years and are re-entering the workforce or you've had half a dozen jobs in the past three years, you can present issues such as these in ways that are more palatable to potential employers. This doesn't mean you'll be saying you were CEO of a Fortune 500 company when you were really sitting on a beach in Belize; rather, you'll be accounting for your experience in a way that still presents you as a strong candidate for the job.

Remember, the purpose of a résumé is to get an interview. Once you're sitting in a room with a hiring manager, you have a chance to explain your situation and address any questions about your track record.

FIRST PERSON DISASTER STORY

Résumé Overkill

I met a woman at a cocktail party who works for a prominent advertising agency. When I mentioned that I was looking for a job in advertising she told me to send her a copy of my résumé. The next day I sat down at my computer and drafted two résumés: one indicating I was interested in a copywriter position and another listing my objective as an account manager position. Since I hadn't really made up my mind which direction better suited me, I e-mailed her both and suggested she pass them on to the appropriate departments. I was mortified to get an e-mail back saying I should figure out what I want to do before getting back in touch. I thought I was being savvy, but clearly I should have sent just one résumé and mentioned in my cover letter that I was interested in two areas.

Justine H., Santa Fe, New Mexico

ASK THE EXPERTS

I was fired from a job for poor performance. Is it better not to list that position on my résumé?

That depends. If you were with the company for more than a year, excluding the job creates a problematic gap on your résumé. Also, if you skip that job on your résumé and are hired by another company, it may come out later that you left out information that might have influenced the company's decision to hire you—which could get you fired. But if the job only lasted a few months—or you feel really strongly about not mentioning it—leave it out. Title the employment section of your résumé Relevant Experience (and not Work History) to indicate that it's a selective listing of the jobs you have held.

My last boss didn't like me and demoted me, hoping I would quit—which I eventually did. Can I list my initial job title on my résumé or do I have to list the lower title as well?

The best solution is to list both job titles after the company name, then describe your accomplishments in one paragraph or a bulleted list (rather than listing your contributions according to each job title). That way, you are being honest about the positions you held, but you don't have to draw attention to which job you had first.

little or no experience

Landing that first job

Whether you're a recent graduate or simply don't have very much experience, there are lots of ways to fill out your résumé. Here are some tips for playing up other skills and accomplishments to land that all-important first job.

■ **Draw on experience besides paid work.**
If you've only had a couple of jobs during school, fill out your Experience section by listing volunteer positions or extracurricular activities (Treasurer, Spanish Club; Representative, Student Council; Assistant Editor, Yearbook; Volunteer, Freshman Orientation; or Captain, Swim Team).

■ **Use a functional or hybrid résumé format.**
If you have only one or two positions to list on your résumé, consider drawing attention to your skills rather than your job titles by using a functional or hybrid format. (See example, opposite page.)

■ **Add a section listing computer or language skills.**
Recent graduates are often more knowledgeable about computers and technology than older candidates—and frequently have foreign language skills that more seasoned workers have long forgotten. Show off your knowledge of computer programs and French in a separate Skills section.

■ **When all else fails, list schoolwork.**
If you're still having trouble filling the page, list academic coursework or special projects related to your job objective.

Should you list your G.P.A.?

Only list your grade point average if it's high enough to serve as an accomplishment. For some technical careers, that might be 3.4 and above; for others, the cutoff might be higher. Use your judgment.

Tamara Jenkins

492 Myrtle Avenue, #5C
Columbus, OH 43210
tjenkins@webmail.net 292-555-8743

OBJECTIVE
A position in sales or marketing with a retail clothing company.

EDUCATION
Ohio State University, B.A., English, 2002
G.P.A.: 3.75 overall

EXPERIENCE
Ohio State University Bookstore, Sales Associate, Columbus, Ohio 2000–present

Sales
   Supervise clothing and accessories department for campus bookstore (promoted to
   supervisory duties after one year of employment). Track inventory, schedule sales clerks,
   and help customers with purchase decisions while monitoring and training employees on
   the sales floor.

Marketing
   Create window and in-store displays for clothing and accessories; Homecoming window
   display contributed to sellout of special event T-shirt during reunion weekend.

Butterfly Boutique, Sales Assistant, Toledo, Ohio Summers, 2000 & 2001

Assisted customers with purchases, operated cash register, and monitored dressing rooms
for local outlet of national retail chain. Invited to return as a seasonal employee the following summer.

The Parrot, Advertising Sales, Columbus, Ohio 1999–2000

Sold classified advertisements for campus newspaper; recruited eight new advertisers in
clothing and sporting goods categories.

SKILLS
Fluent in Spanish (completed overseas study program in Madrid, fall semester, 2001).

Computer graphics skills include Illustrator, PageMaker, QuarkXPress, and Photoshop;
experienced at shooting and editing digital photographs.

employment gaps

**Make your time
away work for you**

Thanks to a more volatile job market and an increasing tendency for workers to take some time away from the workforce for personal reasons, employment gaps no longer carry the stigma they once did among employers. In fact, it's more and more common for résumés to have one or two gaps between jobs.

Still, any holes in your work record require some finessing when you're writing your résumé. You want to demonstrate that you used your time away from the 9-to-5 workweek constructively, focusing attention on the class you took to update your computer skills rather than giving the impression you spent your time watching daytime TV or playing golf.

1. The easiest way to address a brief period away from work is to close short gaps by listing employment in years, not months. Eliminate months from your work experience, and a short gap no longer shows up:

> **Dental Hygienist, Downtown Dental Clinic 12/2000–present**
> **Dental Hygienist, Simon Martin, D.D.S. 3/98–4/2000**
> **vs.**
> **Dental Hygienist, Downtown Dental Clinic 2000–present**
> **Dental Hygienist, Simon Martin, D.D.S. 1998–2000**

2. Account for longer gaps by listing volunteer work, internships, consulting projects, or study (give a short explanation if they relate to your job objective):

> **Peace Corps Volunteer**   2001–2003
>
> **Marketing and Public
> Relations Strategist**   2000–2001

3. Use a functional résumé (see page 16) to de-emphasize time off that was spent on activities unrelated to work (in your Work History section briefly list what you were doing during the gap):

WORK HISTORY

Media Planner, Day Advertising, Los Angeles	2001–2002
Independent travel	1999–2000
Account Manager, Moonbeam Media, New York	1998–1999

4. Save detailed explanations for an interview or cover letter. You don't have to explain everything on your résumé; just try to account for a break in your employment history in a way that won't disqualify you from consideration for a job.

5. Don't reveal unflattering reasons for being out of work. If you were unemployed, in a rehabilitation program, or out of the job market for other reasons you'd rather not discuss, don't list those explanations on your résumé. Find another way to account for your time away from work. If you were recovering from an illness, think twice about stating that on your résumé—employers might assume you are still unhealthy and will ask for a lot of time off.

6. If possible, include temporary positions to account for your time between jobs. Group them under a heading with a short descriptive statement and then list three or four firms and dates of service below.

TEMPORARY POSITIONS
Ongoing short-term assignments at major Fortune 1000 companies
Planet Technology (2001–present)
Stillwater Consulting (2002–present)
International Machine Corp. (2002–present)

re-entering the workforce

How to handle an extended gap in employment

Whether you took several years off to raise a family, write a novel, or travel the world, you'll need to address that extended gap on your résumé. How you should handle it depends on a number of variables:

■ Do you have previous work experience?

If you worked for many years or held several jobs before taking time off, a standard chronological résumé focusing on your previous experience may be your best option. If you have limited prior work experience, a functional résumé will let you focus more on your skills.

■ How long were you out of the workforce?

If you only took a year off, you may not need to mention what you were doing while away. But if you were out of the workforce for two or more years, it's best to account for your time off.

■ Did you work part-time?

If you worked part-time or did some consulting from home, list that as you would any other job, especially if the work is related to your objective. (If it isn't, list it under Other Experience, with minimal explanation.)

■ Did you do any volunteer work?

Volunteer work still counts as experience—especially if you used skills related to your field, like budgeting, fund-raising, or event planning. If your volunteer work involved a big commitment, list it with your other work experience. If not, you should still include it in another section to account for a gap in your work history.

SKILLS AND EXPERIENCE

Customer Service

■ Assisted passengers with security, comfort, and information needs as flight attendant with major airline; received customer service award for attentiveness to special needs passengers.

■ Helped library patrons locate books, find reference materials, and learn how to use computers and the Internet for research purposes.

Fund-raising

■ Solicited $10,500 in donations for county garden club project to landscape school grounds.

■ Organized benefit for local library, raising $15,000 for new computer equipment.

WORK HISTORY

United Airlines, Flight Attendant	1994–1998
Grass Valley Public Library, Assistant Librarian	1999–2000
Antrim County Garden Club, Vice President	2000–present
Stay-at-Home Parent	2000–present

Ways to describe time raising kids . . .
Stay-at-Home Parent
Full-time Parent
Family Child Care
Family Caregiver

. . . or traveling
Freelance Photographer
Study Abroad
Independent Travel
Spanish-Language Student

making a career transition

Paving the way for a change

Most people change careers several times during their working lives—so you can too. That said, simply retooling your résumé is often not enough to land you a job in a completely unrelated line of work. Chances are, you'll need to get some experience or training in order to make the transition (see box on opposite page for a few ideas). Once you have some experience to work with, revise your résumé to persuade potential employers you can make the leap from point A to point B by:

■ **Listing relevant work first**
The first thing a hiring manager sees on your résumé should relate to the job you want. List relevant experience first—under a heading like Related Experience—even if it's an internship or unpaid work.

■ **Highlighting transferable skills**
Focus on transferable skills as you list your accomplishments in other jobs. Your experience making sales presentations to large groups is useful if you want to be a speechwriter; list it under a heading like Presentations instead of Sales. Similarly, fluency in more than one language may bump you to the head of the pack if the company you are applying to is based overseas, requires extensive international travel, or works with foreign clients or partners. To highlight your ability, list it separately under the heading Language Skills. Or, if interacting with the media will be an important aspect of the corporate communications job you are applying for and you have represented your firm by making television appearances or doing radio interviews, list these activities separately under the heading of Media Appearances.

■ Downplaying unrelated experience

Not all work experience is equal. You may have spent twice as long as a landscape architect than you did as an interior designer, but if you'd rather be working with fabric swatches than flower beds, devote more space to your interior design work.

■ Using your summary to reposition yourself

A Summary of Qualifications or Profile section is particularly important for career changers (see page 36). Use it to highlight skills related to your objective and to identify yourself as someone qualified for the job you want.

■ Considering a functional résumé format

A functional résumé (see page 16) lets you shift the focus from job titles to skills. For that reason, it's often a good choice for those looking to change careers.

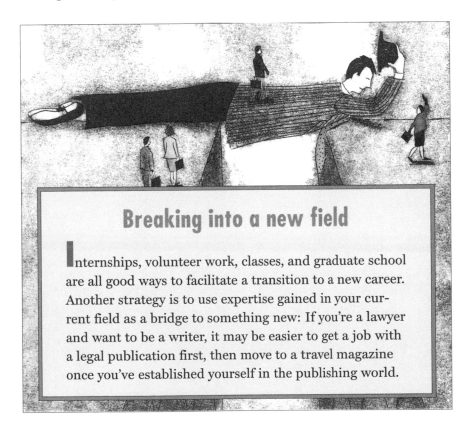

Breaking into a new field

Internships, volunteer work, classes, and graduate school are all good ways to facilitate a transition to a new career. Another strategy is to use expertise gained in your current field as a bridge to something new: If you're a lawyer and want to be a writer, it may be easier to get a job with a legal publication first, then move to a travel magazine once you've established yourself in the publishing world.

a single employer

Make your stable
track record work
for you

Being a stable employee with a long commitment to one company goes in and out of favor on the job market. Regardless of the prevailing mood, you can turn your longtime employment into an asset by presenting it as a positive.

- List your titles separately, highlighting different skills and accomplishments below each job.

- Omit the total number of years you worked for the company; list years for each position instead.

- If your title did not change, divide your experience at the company into several sections, with headings that describe your skills like Research or Account Management.

- If you were never promoted, demonstrate progress by mentioning increased responsibilities and bonuses (just the fact that you were awarded a bonus—not specific numbers).

- Mention any training or courses you have taken to show that you have been developing your skills.

- Be prepared to discuss in an interview why you are leaving the company now. (You may also want to address this topic in your cover letter.)

Résumé Excerpt: One Employer

PROFESSIONAL EXPERIENCE

ABC Foods   East Hanover, NJ

Senior Business Analyst   1998–present

- Analyze and monitor activity of multiple brands to track progress against company sales and profit objectives; met or exceeded goals in 9 of the previous 12 quarters.

- Assist in the development of strategic plans for assigned brands; work on cross-functional team to identify new opportunities and anticipate challenges.

- Promoted to position after completing M.B.A. concurrent with previous job.

Market Research Manager   1994–95

- Supervised market research for Crunch cereal brands, resulting in a major repackaging effort to increase appeal to the youth market.

- Conducted focus groups in multiple cities, analyzed data, and compiled reports for brand managers; recommended new survey technique implemented throughout department.

- Identified opportunity to move into growing multigrain cereal market based on surveys indicating this preference among 18- to 34-year-olds.

Marketing Services Assistant   1992–94

- Devised survey questionnaires, handled logistics for focus groups, and provided preliminary statistical analysis of data for market research department.

- Conducted research for supervisors on packaged food industry trends.

too many jobs

Good news. It's much more acceptable than it used to be to have changed jobs often. Even so, there is still a fine line between having a diverse set of job titles on your résumé and being perceived as a worker who can't settle down (often referred to as a job hopper). If you've moved around a lot, assess how mobility is viewed in your industry and then decide how many jobs to list on your résumé—and how many to leave off.

Remember, your résumé doesn't have to tell your whole story; sometimes, less is more. Here are five ways to downplay a work history with too many jobs.

1. List dates of employment by year, not month (i.e., 1990–91, not 11/90–2/91).

2. Consider using a functional résumé, especially if you have had lots of similar jobs.

3. Only include jobs that support your objective. (List them under a header like Relevant Experience to indicate that it's a selective listing of your employment history.)

4. Leave out jobs you held early in your career, especially if they are unrelated to your objective or are similar to more recent positions you have held.

5. Use your cover letter or Summary of Qualifications section to dispel any perception that you have a commitment problem.

ASK THE EXPERTS

I worked for a temporary services agency for years, so I've had dozens of jobs. How should I handle that on my résumé?

List the name of the agency as your employer, along with the total number of years you have worked for the company and a general description of the type of work you have done. Choose two or three assignments to highlight below that—ideally, longer-term positions that are related to your objective. Describe those positions as you would any other job—by listing the name of the employer and your accomplishments.

I'm a self-employed film and video editor, so I've had a mix of short- and long-term projects. How do I capture my wide range of experience without looking flighty?

Find a way to organize your experience according to specific categories—like film projects, television projects, and corporate work. Or list longer-term projects as you would any other job, then list your shorter assignments under a separate heading, like Additional Experience. The goal is to find a way to divide your experience into several coherent categories so employers aren't overwhelmed by a lengthy list of jobs.

I was laid off twice during the collapse of the Internet bubble. Should I say on my résumé that the firms I worked for folded?

With the recent volatility in the job market, most employers understand that workers lose jobs through layoffs or company closings through no fault of their own. Even so, it's best not to draw attention to why you left the company on your résumé; you can discuss questions like that more effectively in an interview. Also, since you were laid off twice, some employers might assume you exercised poor judgment by picking an unstable company after being burned once. If one of your jobs was very short-term, consider leaving it off your résumé entirely.

former business owner

Sometimes you need
to downplay self-
employment

Having owned your own business gives you terrific experience. But when making the transition back to working for someone else, you may run into certain negative perceptions out in the job market.

For starters, the fact that you are looking for a job implies that going solo didn't exactly work out. That may or may not be true in your case, but be prepared to explain why you are looking for a staff job—either in your cover letter or an interview—when the question comes up.

In addition, employers in more traditional fields might be less inclined to hire an individual who has spent a long time being his

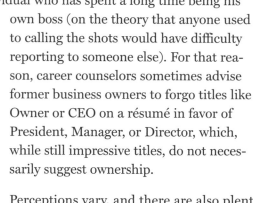

own boss (on the theory that anyone used to calling the shots would have difficulty reporting to someone else). For that reason, career counselors sometimes advise former business owners to forgo titles like Owner or CEO on a résumé in favor of President, Manager, or Director, which, while still impressive titles, do not necessarily suggest ownership.

Perceptions vary, and there are also plenty of employers who value entrepreneurship and all of the qualities it takes to launch and manage a business. So use your judgment about whether to be up front about your ownership role. When in doubt, play it down on your résumé. At the interview you can gauge the attitude of the hiring manager before discussing the topic further.

Timothy Hall

112-02 33rd St., Brooklyn, NY 54321

718-555-8978 • thall@thall.net

SUMMARY OF SKILLS

Award-winning film editor with extensive experience using state-of-the art digital technology. Highly skilled in digital video editing as well as cutting-edge animation applications.

APPLICATIONS AND SYSTEMS

• Comfortable with PC, Mac, and Avid systems

• Proficient using Pro Tools, Flash, Adobe Photoshop, Strata Vision 3-D, Adobe Premier, Adobe Illustrator

• Considerable expertise with 3-D and 2-D animation

WORK EXPERIENCE

2001–Present, Film and Video Editor
Video Graphic, AC/DF Media, Open Broadcasting, Wink Worldwide
New York, NY

• Create and edit short animation sequences for use in interactive commercials.

• Produce numerous animation sequences for use in interactive ads.

1998–2001 Video Graphic Artist
ZBS, New York, NY

• Produced and edited short animation sequences for use in commercials.

• Retouched still video pictures for use in broadcast video.

• Completed linear editing for a wide array of projects.

• Researched and implemented use of various software applications, improved efficiencies in production, and built substantial savings for the company.

• Created and produced 11 commercials and numerous Chyron animation sequences.

EDUCATION

New York University, Tisch School of Arts, B.F.A., 1997

Writing Guidelines

■ If you owned your own business, play up the skills you have honed with appropriate skills sections rather than your title of President or CEO.

■ Employ descriptive titles like Film and Video Editor or Advertising Copywriter rather than more generic titles like Communications Consultant.

■ Some people have a skeptical view of the role of a consultant. Unless you are applying to a management consulting firm, describe yourself with a skill-based term like Video Editor or Corporate Communications Strategist.

■ If you wore many hats in your self-employment years, emphasize the projects you completed that relate to the position you want.

■ Don't lead with the word *freelance* or *self-employed*. Emphasize what you did rather than the fact that you were a freelancer or self-employed by listing a traditional title on your résumé and then subtly mentioning that you worked for multiple clients.

does age matter?

Although it's illegal for employers to discriminate against employees or job applicants because of age, managers generally have a certain age range in mind when they are looking to hire someone. Their preconception is based on factors such as how much experience they expect candidates to have, whether the position involves managing other employees, and how much the job pays.

Because of these expectations—which may be conscious or subconscious—it's wise to make sure your résumé positions you in the age range you think employers are looking for. Usually, you can get some sense from the description of the position and type of candidate the company is seeking. For example, a magazine that advertises an entry-level position for an editorial assistant probably expects to receive piles of résumés from recent college graduates, while the same publication hiring an editor-in-chief would be looking for someone with a lot more experience—someone older, in other words.

The point is not to misrepresent yourself; it's to make sure your résumé gets through the screening process. Once you show up for an interview, you have a chance to convince the company you're right for the job, regardless of your birth date.

Giving Your Résumé Some Age

On a résumé, adding years to your age is more difficult than taking a few years away. But there are a few things you can do to eliminate a "youthful" feeling from your résumé.

■ Don't list the date you graduated from college or received any graduate degrees. (However, you may have to provide these later so that your education information can be verified.)

■ Title your work experience Related Experience or Relevant Experience, which gives the impression it is only a partial listing of the positions you have held during your career.

■ Leave out any positions that seem collegiate—like a job at a university bookstore or college newspaper.

■ Even if you go by a nickname like Billy or Cathy, use a formal name like William or Catherine on your résumé.

Making Your Résumé "Younger"

■ List only your most recent work experience; make sure the years you worked in those positions add up to the amount of experience that seems appropriate for the job opening.

■ If you want to include more "ancient" work experience because it relates to your objective, just list the most relevant positions you have held throughout your career and call the section Related Experience.

■ Don't list dates you received any college degrees.

now what do I do?

Answers to common questions

My current job title is administrative assistant, but that's so vague it doesn't give any indication of the type of work I do. Is it okay to use a more descriptive job title?

Since a potential employer might call your company to verify your employment status, it's best to list your title accurately so you don't seem to be misrepresenting yourself. In this case, one solution would be to list a two-part title, one that accurately reflects what you do and one that gives your precise job title (e.g., Marketing Coordinator/Administrative Assistant). Or add your department after your title (e.g., Administrative Assistant, Marketing).

My résumé doesn't list data that would give away my age, but an interviewer asked how old I was. Is that allowed?

The **Age Discrimination in Employment Act,** a federal law prohibiting discrimination based on age, does not specifically prohibit an employer from asking an applicant's age or date of birth. However, employers still have to be careful about asking that question because it can indicate a possible intent to discriminate based on age. If you don't want to answer, say something vague like, "I'm in my thirties." That will usually deter further probing.

After interviewing at a firm and not receiving an offer, I heard from a friend who works there that my age was a factor. What should I do?

If you believe you were discriminated against because of your age, the U.S. Equal Employment Opportunity Commission has information about relevant laws and how to protect your rights (**www.eeoc.gov** or 1-800-669-4000).

Can I ask a recruiter to let me revise my résumé each time she sends it to a potential employer?

Most recruiters probably won't give you this option. But they usually call prospective applicants to gauge their interest in a particular opening before submitting a résumé to an employer. So if it's a job that really appeals to you—or you have new information to add to your résumé—it's worth asking if you can submit a revised version.

Which is worse—leaving a gap on your résumé or indicating that you took a year off to travel?

That depends on your field and the company you are applying to. Some employers might think an applicant who didn't work for a year was unmotivated, while others might value skills you developed on the road—particularly if the job you want involves lots of travel. Research the employer and use your judgment.

I worked for technology companies in the late 1990s and had many employers and many job titles at each company. Should I downplay my promotions?

Technology companies gained a reputation for crazy job titles, like Director of Fun, and for promoting young workers to positions like Executive Vice President long before an employee would earn that title in another industry. If you think your job title or promotions will raise eyebrows at the company you are applying to, it may be prudent to list a more modest title—or list two positions instead of four.

Now where do I go?

WEB SITES

Equal Employment Opportunity Commission
www.eeoc.gov or 800-669-4000
Information about workplace discrimination.

FindLaw
www.findlaw.com
Internet legal resource.

Campus Career Center
www.campuscareercenter.com
Recruiting service aimed at college graduates.

BOOKS

Real Résumés for Career Changers: Actual Résumés and Cover Letters
by Anne McKinney (Editor)

Change Your Job, Change Your Life, 8th Edition
by Ron Krannich
Advice on changing careers.

101 Best Résumés for Grads
by Jay A. Block and Michael Betrus
Sample résumés and advice for college graduates.

Formatting the final version

The goal is to make your résumé easy to read, whether on paper or a computer screen.

an electronic era

While it's still important to have a version of your résumé that looks impressive on paper, these days you will probably spend more time preparing your document so it can be sent by e-mail or submitted to a Web page than adding design elements like shaded boxes and horizontal lines to make the printed page look pretty.

That's because much of the formatting of a document—like bold and italics—disappears once the text is copied and pasted into an e-mail message. You may be using an e-mail software program that can transmit or receive formatted text, but you never know what program your recipient is using. So even if your résumé looks fine in your outgoing e-mail message, it might arrive looking like gibberish on the other end.

To prevent that travesty, you'll need to consider how you plan to submit your résumé before making choices about design elements like text style, layout, and use of special characters. This chapter explains how to adapt your résumé for the electronic era, plus offers some general design principles that apply to both computer and print submissions.

One Résumé, Many Outlets

■ **Printed on paper**

Paper isn't obsolete—you'll still need a print version of your résumé to take with you to interviews, or to send by fax, or even via old-fashioned postal mail.

■ **Sent via e-mail**

E-mail has rapidly become the most common way of sending résumés to employers. The résumé is either pasted into the body of a message or sent as an **attachment**, a document in a Microsoft Word or other word processing format that can be digitally "paper clipped" to an e-mail message.

■ **Submitted to a Web form**

Some employers have Web sites with electronic forms that job seekers can fill out to apply for open positions (these are often called **résumé builders**). In some cases, this involves typing information like your name, address, and work experience into separate boxes; at other times it involves copying and pasting your entire résumé into one field. These forms are also used by Web sites that post positions available with many different employers (see page 110).

■ **Posted on a Web page**

Internet users who have their own Web sites sometimes post their résumés on their site. In this case, the résumé must be formatted using Hypertext Markup Language (HTML), the coding used to display information on the Web.

■ **Scanned into a database**

Some employers still take paper résumés and put them into a scanner, a machine that looks like a photocopier and makes a digital version of a print document. Though this process is less common now that so many résumés are submitted electronically, résumés that are going to be scanned need to be formatted so the scanner can read them.

basic layout principles

**Design an
inviting page**

Whether you're sending your résumé electronically or printing it out, you should keep in mind certain factors about the layout—the way information is organized on the page. The goal is to make your résumé easy to read, whether on paper or a computer screen.

No matter how you are submitting your résumé, it's important that your document have plenty of white space—blank areas that separate blocks of information. To make sure you have enough white space, leave two or three blank lines after your contact information and between sections like your Summary of Qualifications and Work Experience.

For a print résumé, set your margins—the white space around the edges of the page—at no less than an inch on the sides and at least half an inch on the top and bottom of the page. (See page 167 for how to set your margins when sending a résumé via e-mail.)

Indenting certain information—such as your list of accomplishments below each job title—lets you set apart blocks of text, which generally makes a page easier to read. Using bullets, asterisks, or hyphens at the beginning of each accomplishment also helps set apart different ideas.

Distinguish section headers (Objective and Work Experience, for example) from other text by making that text bold or using larger letters than the text that follows or, for résumés that will be sent by e-mail, using all capital letters.

½-inch border

Nick Peluzzi
36 Ashland Avenue, #3A
Denver, CO 98765
npeluzzi@webmail.net
321-555-4321

2-line space

OBJECTIVE: Position as an on-site computer support specialist.

SUMMARY OF QUALIFICATIONS

- Eight years of experience troubleshooting for desktop and laptop computers made by multiple manufacturers, including Windows and Apple machines.

1-inch border

- Strong knowledge of most business software programs, including Microsoft's Office suite; Outlook and Eudora e-mail packages; PowerPoint presentation software; Adobe Acrobat; and many design and illustration programs.

1-inch border

- Patient yet fast worker with a remarkable ability to calm agitated computer users; comfortable working in fast-paced environments.

Bold section head

WORK EXPERIENCE

Director of Management Information Systems, Petite Publishing, 1999–present, Boston, MA

- Provided technical support for hardware that included 200-plus computers, two Windows NT Servers, and one SCO UNIX server.

- Evaluated, purchased, and installed software and provided technical support for programs, including Microsoft Office and Outlook, and Adobe Photoshop and Illustrator.

Systems Analyst, Catalyst Computer Corporation, 1995–1998, Andover, MA

Bulleted item

- Managed purchasing, maintenance, and support of information technology system for $200 million business.

- Wrote accounting programs still in use for invoicing and tracking accounts receivable.

EDUCATION

Syracuse University, Management Information Systems, B.S.

½-inch border

choosing a typeface

When choosing a typeface or font—design terms for the appearance of letters—the goal is to select a style commonly installed on most computers and easy to read. Typefaces come in two types: serif and sans serif. A serif font, like the one used for the text of this book, has letters that have little flourishes where the lines end. A sans serif font has letters made of simple lines.

Serif fonts are considered easier to read—which is why most books and newspapers use them, and why you too should choose a serif font for your résumé. A few common serif fonts are Times New Roman, Palatino, and Courier. (Examples of sans serif fonts include Helvetica, Arial, and Futura.)

Besides choosing the type of font, you also select the type size. In general, it is best to use a font size no smaller than 10 points for the main text of your résumé (12 points is a good choice). For your name and section headers, you might want to use a larger font (though for a résumé sent via e-mail, you should just use one font size). When faxing a résumé use a 12-point type size, since the type will be reduced during transmission, making 10-point type difficult to read.

Finally, for a printed résumé, you can also make some text **bold**, *italic*, or <u>underlined</u> (like section headers or company names). However, since underlined text can blur after a document has been faxed or photocopied, bold is usually a safer choice.

Keep it simple

Don't get too creative with your font choices. Changing fonts within your document, or using too many different styles or sizes, can be distracting to read. Pick one or two fonts or sizes and stick with them.

Serif Fonts

12 point Times New Roman
11 point Times New Roman
10 point Times New Roman

12 point Palatino
11 point Palatino
10 point Palatino

12 point Courier
11 point Courier
10 point Courier

Sans Serif Fonts

12 point Helvetica
11 point Helvetica
10 point Helvetica

12 point Arial
11 point Arial
10 point Arial

12 point Futura
11 point Futura
10 point Futura

Changing the Font

The following instructions explain changing font style and size in Microsoft Word (most word processing programs operate in a similar fashion):

1. To change all the text on the page, select Edit from the toolbar and then choose Select All. (If you just want to change some text, use your mouse to highlight the text you want changed—click and hold the mouse button at the beginning of your selection and release it when you've highlighted the text you want changed.) The text you've chosen should appear highlighted.

2. With the text still highlighted, click the Format menu and choose Font. A new window will open.

3. Within that new window, the first box on the left allows you to change the font. Click and hold the bar between the two arrows and move it up or down to view the font choices available on your computer. Once you've found the one you want, click it once to select it. Your choice should appear in the Preview window on the bottom of the page.

4. If you also want to change the font size, follow the same instructions using the box in the right of the window and select the font size you want.

5. If you want to change the font style (e.g., make a header bold), use the box in the middle of the window to select that option.

6. When you're finished, click the OK button. The font in your document will change automatically.

formatting for print

Lines and bullets
can be effective
design elements

For the printed version of your résumé, you should pay more attention to your document's design. You don't have to hire a graphic designer to make your résumé look sharp—adding a few simple elements can be enough to really spruce up the page.

Adding Lines

One easy way to give your page a more polished look is by inserting a horizontal line that separates your contact information from the rest of your résumé (see below). You can also add a vertical line down the left side of the page—but don't get too carried away or the lines will be distracting to your reader.

Catherine Phillips
325 Willow Road, Chicago, IL 12345
cphillips@webmail.net   312-555-8756

Inserting Bullets

Another easy option is to use bullets or other symbols to highlight certain sentences or phrases (like your list of accomplishments or Summary of Qualifications). To insert a bullet using Microsoft Word in Windows, select the Format menu, then Bullets and Numbering. On a Macintosh, press the Option key and the 8 key simultaneously.

SUMMARY OF QUALIFICATIONS

- 12 years of experience designing, installing, and maintaining aquariums

- Clients range from large corporate offices to residential enthusiasts

Inserting Lines in Microsoft Word

1. With your Microsoft Word document open, choose the Format menu, then select Borders and Shading. A new window will open on the top of your page.

2. In the left column of the window, select the Custom option, then in the middle column choose a style and a width for your line. In the right column of the window, choose a button to indicate where the line should be placed.

3. The preview graphics on the right side of the window will show where the line will appear in your document. Click OK and the line will automatically be inserted in your résumé.

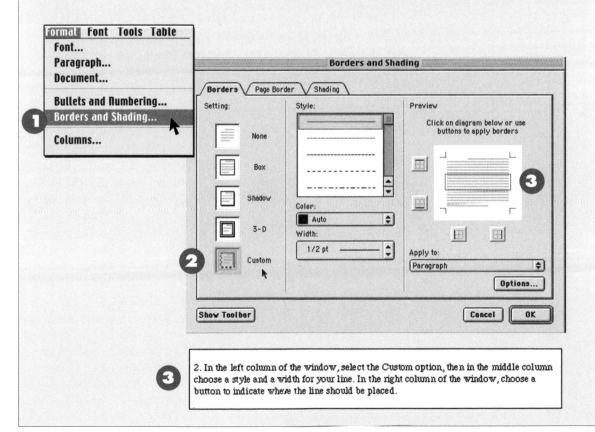

2. In the left column of the window, select the Custom option, then in the middle column choose a style and a width for your line. In the right column of the window, choose a button to indicate where the line should be placed.

saving space

How to trim your
résumé to a
single page

Fitting everything onto one page has become less of an issue as more and more résumés are submitted electronically. Still, there are times when you need a printout of your résumé, and unless you've been working for decades, you'll want to keep it to one page. If you find your text spilling over onto a second page, here are some tips on saving space.

Change the font

Some fonts (typefaces) take up less space than others, even when the point size remains the same. Times New Roman is a good choice if you are trying to fit your résumé onto one page. You can also try using a smaller font size, but anything less than 10 points can be difficult to read.

Adjust your margins

It's best to maintain 1-inch **margins**—the space around the edges of the page—on the left and right sides, but you can gain a few extra lines by setting your top and bottom margins to 0.5 or 0.75 inches.

Eliminate "widows"

You can save a line or two on your résumé by looking for **widows**— a copyediting term for places where a sentence runs from one line to the next at the end of a paragraph or section, leaving only a word or part of a word on the last line. Find a way to edit the sentence so that it ends on the previous line.

Condense your contact information

If your phone number and e-mail address are listed on separate lines, you can gain space by putting them on the same line, separated by a tab or several spaces. The same goes for the parts of your address.

Adjusting the Margins in Microsoft Word

1. With your résumé open in Microsoft Word, select the Format menu, then Document.

2. A new window will open up. If the Margins tab is not already selected, click on it.

3. Use the arrow keys to increase the top, bottom, left, or right margins. A preview graphic on the right side of the window will show what your document will look like with the margins you have selected.

4. When you have set the margins you want, click the OK button.

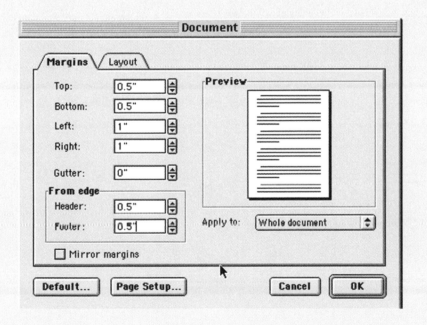

formatting for e-mail

Fancy effects will disappear in an e-mail

When you submit your résumé by e-mail, your formatting options are limited by the fact that many e-mail programs can only handle plain text—a document format that lacks bold, italics, underlines, multiple font sizes, and other fancy effects.

Also referred to as ASCII text, which stands for American Standard Code for Information Interchange, a plain text document is something of a lowest common denominator in the computer world because it can be read by nearly all computer systems.

Plain text format is primarily used when sending a résumé within an e-mail message (rather than in a separate file as an e-mail attachment). Although you can use a regular, formatted document when you send your résumé as an attachment, most employers prefer résumés to be pasted directly into an e-mail message. (See page 168 for more about e-mail attachments.)

Having a plain text version of your résumé is also useful when you are submitting your résumé to a job database—a Web site that posts job listings from employers and the résumés of people seeking employment. (For more about these sites, see page 110.)

FIRST PERSON DISASTER STORY

Test Run

I'd been very industrious with my job search for more than a month, e-mailing several résumés each day. Yet, I wasn't having much luck—in fact, I hadn't gotten a single response. Finally, a friend offered to take a look at my résumé, so I e-mailed it off to her. Moments later she called to tell me that it was completely indecipherable. That was when I discovered that all my careful formatting—bullet points, underlines, and a sharp-looking typeface—morphed into gobbledygook when sent by e-mail. I started using a plain text résumé the next day and have since gotten a few bites. Wish I'd thought to run an e-mail test a little sooner!

Jennifer L., Highland Lakes, New Jersey

 **S**TEP BY STEP

Saving Your Résumé as Plain Text

1. To convert a regular document into plain text, select the File menu, then choose Save As.

2. A new window will open on top of your document. At the bottom of the window, change the File Name to a different name, like "PlainTextRésumé."

3. Next to the field that says Save as Type, click and hold the arrow until a menu selection appears, then select Text Only. Click the OK button.

4. On screen, your document will still look the same. You have to close your document and then open the plain text document—calling it up by the new name you chose—in order to see any difference in the format.

5. Once you've opened the plain text version of your résumé, you'll notice that much of the formatting has been erased. In some cases, you'll want to replace a missing element with an alternative that is acceptable in plain text documents, like several spaces where an indent used to be, or dashes or asterisks where bullet points were.

résumé databases

Electronic files help
match up companies
and job seekers

For employers, one of the main advantages of digital résumés is that they can be stored in a résumé database—the electronic equivalent of a filing cabinet that is much easier to search. When résumés are saved in a database, hiring managers can use their computers to search for particular keywords—words or phrases like "sales manager," "pharmaceutical representative," or "banking"—to find candidates with specific qualifications.

There are two types of résumé databases: those maintained internally by companies to store résumés they have received directly from applicants, and those maintained by employment services that match job seekers with openings at multiple companies.

Career Web sites

There are a wide range of general employment Web sites, focusing on everything from particular professions to special interest groups to geographic regions. Three popular sites to check out are **www.monster.com**, **www.careerbuilder.com**, and **www.hotjobs.com**.

Usually, candidates can submit their résumés for free using an electronic form on the Web site. Often, employers can also post job openings and wait for applicants to respond, or search the résumé database for candidates with certain qualifications (services for which employers usually pay a fee).

Company Web sites

Some companies that have developed more sophisticated Web sites—particularly Internet or technology companies—now ask job seekers to apply for openings by submitting their résumé to an electronic form on the company's site. (Many companies also post openings on their Web site, and request that applicants send their résumés to an e-mail address.)

ASK THE EXPERTS

I'm interested in posting my résumé on a career site. What will I need to do?

Before allowing visitors to post a résumé or apply for job openings, most career Web sites require that you register—fill in a form with contact information and set up a username and password you'll need to remember and use every time you want to access the Web site. Once you have registered, you can add your résumé to the site's database. In most cases, this involves filling in a form—sometimes referred to as a résumé builder—rather than copying and pasting your entire résumé. You'll usually be asked to enter information like your objective, address, desired job, and employment history on a series of screens. You can either cut and paste this information from the plain text version of your résumé or type it in.

How long does it take to post your résumé to a site?

The entire process can take anywhere between 15 minutes and an hour; most sites let you save your data and finish your résumé later, if necessary. (Your résumé does not get added to the site's database until you complete the entire process.)

creating a
database résumé

Preparing your résumé for an electronic file

If you are submitting your résumé to a database, or think it might be saved in one, you'll want to take certain steps to make the process go smoothly—and to ensure that your résumé gets noticed after it has been deposited in the electronic netherworld.

For starters, whether you're e-mailing your résumé or cutting and pasting it into a Web form, you should use a plain text version of your document. (For help saving a document as plain text, see page 109.) Most Web sites that save résumés directly into a database will advise you to eliminate any formatting like bold or italics. But if you are e-mailing your résumé and aren't sure whether it will end up in a database, send a simply formatted version.

To increase the chance that your résumé turns up when employers are searching the database for qualified candidates, make sure you use plenty of **keywords**—words or phrases hiring managers are likely to type into a search field to find appropriate résumés.

For example, someone looking to hire an accountant might search a résumé database for words like "accountant," "C.P.A.," or "certified public accountant." (Whenever possible, list both abbreviations and their equivalent.) The results are typically ranked by the number of keywords each résumé contains, so a résumé that matches all the keywords a hiring manager enters will be listed above one that matches only half the terms.

Keywords can be ...

- Skills (graphic design or sales forecasting)

- Industries (banking or automotive)

- Geographic areas (Chicago or Florida)

- Degrees (M.B.A. or Ph.D.)

- Company names (Microsoft or Merrill Lynch)

Where Do Keywords Go?

There are two ways you can handle keywords: either creating a section titled Keywords on your résumé or sprinkling keywords throughout your document, such as in your Summary of Qualifications, Objective, and Work Experience. If you list your keywords in a separate section, limit yourself to 20 to 30 terms—and skip the Summary or Profile section (to avoid being repetitive).

Résumé with separate keyword section

Aaron Samuels
277 W. 10th Street, 4N   New York, NY 03456
212-555-8769   asamuels@webmail.net

KEYWORDS: editor, copyeditor, managing editor, writer, assignment editor, research, proofreading, features, news, articles, medical, science, health, fitness, freelance writers, layout, photography, design

OBJECTIVE: Editor position at a fitness or health publication.

Résumé with keywords throughout

Keywords are boldfaced here for illustration purposes only—do not boldface them in your résumé.

Aaron Samuels
277 W. 10th Street, 4N   New York, NY 03456
212-555-8769   asamuels@webmail.net

OBJECTIVE: **Editor** position at a **fitness** or **health** publication.

SUMMARY OF QUALIFICATIONS:

■ 15 years of **editorial** experience, including positions as a **managing editor, assignment editor, features editor, copyeditor,** and **writer**

■ Have extensive network of **freelance writers** specializing in **medical, science, health,** and **fitness**

■ Wordsmith who also has an eye for **photography, layout,** and **design**

how scanners work

When companies
convert paper résumés
to digital form

Scanners—devices that look like a miniature version of a photo-copier and can be used to convert paper documents into digital format—are pretty common these days. In fact, many people use them at home to create digital versions of photographs.

In the past, many companies used scanners to create electronic versions of paper résumés. While digital conversion is often unnecessary now that so many résumés are submitted in electronic form, some large or traditional companies still scan résumés submitted by mail. If you think there's a possibility your résumé will be scanned, it's a good idea to find out so that you can make the necessary format changes.

Scanners create an electronic image of a résumé—essentially, a digital snapshot like a photograph. A second process uses what is called **OCR** or **optical character recognition** technology, which turns the image into an electronic text file. The final document can then be saved in a **database**, or virtual filing cabinet, and searched for keywords.

OCR technology is not perfect, however—sometimes it can't "read" the document and ends up introducing errors into the text. That's why you need to format your document to be scanner friendly.

Flatbed scanners look like miniature copy machines. Just put your résumé or picture facedown and presto, copy it into your computer's hard drive.

ASK THE EXPERTS

What do I need to do to prepare my résumé for a scanner?

Because a scanner uses character recognition technology to turn printed pages into electronic text files, you need to make your document easy for the computer to read. Start by printing it on white paper (one side only) and deleting extra design elements, such as lines or shading—indents, tabs, capitals, and centered text are fine. Other measures to take include:

- Using a scannable font (like Palatino, Times New Roman, Courier, or Helvetica)

- Eliminating elaborate formatting (like bold, underlining, and italics), and replacing bullets with dashes or asterisks

- Using a 10- or 12-point font

- Putting each part of your contact information on a separate line

- Not faxing a résumé that will be scanned (faxes blur the text) and not folding a résumé that will be mailed

How do I know if my résumé is going to be saved in a database?

If you are submitting your résumé to a form on a Web site, it will almost invariably be saved in a database. If you are sending your résumé by e-mail, it may or may not be added to a database on the other end. (The same goes for résumés sent by fax or postal mail.) When in doubt, try calling the company and asking.

now what do I do?

How can I find employment Web sites related to my field or focused on my city?

For local job listings, many newspapers post their classified ads on their Web sites and in some cases have partnered with a recruiter or employment service to offer more elaborate career services online. For employment services dedicated to a specific industry or field, start with a trade association, which may offer job listings on its own Web site or link to one that does. You can also try using an Internet search engine and entering the name of your field and the phrase "job listings."

My e-mail program lets me send messages containing bold text, different font sizes, and other basic formatting. Is it okay to use these features to make my résumé look better?

Even though your e-mail program lets you use formatted text, you never know what software someone else is using on the other end. The recipient's e-mail program or Internet service provider may not be able to read formatted text—in which case your message will arrive with indecipherable coding or strange extra characters. It's better to play it safe and send plain text.

Is it better to put keywords in a separate section or use them throughout my résumé?

Putting **keywords**—words hiring managers are likely to type into the search field of a career Web site to find appropriate résumés—into a separate section is most useful when a computer rather than a human being will be reading your résumé first. So unless you know your résumé is going directly into a database, i.e., you are submitting it to a career Web site, you're better off sprinkling keywords throughout your document.

Can I update my résumé once I've submitted it to a Web site?

Most career Web sites that list job openings from multiple employers let you make changes to your résumé at any time. It is less common for company Web sites that have résumé submission forms to offer this feature (though you can always submit a new résumé and see if you get a response).

Some of the companies I've applied to offer both an e-mail address and a mailing address. I've submitted my plain text résumé; should I send a hard copy as well?

It's a good practice to follow up your e-résumé submission with a printed copy by snail mail (U.S. Postal Service). It may seem repetitious but it's good insurance—and gives you a chance to get a beautifully formatted résumé on nice 20-pound bond paper to the hiring manager. But be sure to note in your cover letter that you are following up your e-mailed submission with a printed version, so it won't look like you're bombarding them with submissions.

Now where do I go?

WEB SITES

www.monster.com
Post your résumé and search through job listings.

www.careerbuilder.com
Classified ads from media companies and a résumé database.

www.hotjobs.com
Another site with general job listings and a résumé database.

www.hoovers.com
Find Web addresses and information about public and private companies.

BOOKS

Career Xroads 2002
by Gerry Crispin & Mark Miller
A directory of job search, career, and résumé Web sites.

Job Searching Online for Dummies, 2nd Edition
by Pam Dixon
Advice on finding and applying for jobs online.

The Jobsearch Manual
by Linda Aspey
Offers techniques for targeting employers and applying for jobs through the Internet.

Writing a cover letter

A cover letter reveals things
about your style and personality
that may clinch whether
or not you get a call.

what is a cover letter?

Your résumé is done and it's wonderful. Good for you! Now what?
If you know people who are waiting for it, should you just send it
off with a little note saying "Here it is"? Probably not a good idea.
A better idea would be to take the time to write an interview-
clinching cover letter—the one- or two-paragraph letter that sets
the stage for your résumé. Some people think of a cover letter as
something employers will breeze right past. Not true.

Plenty of employers follow the predictable order—first reading the
cover letter and then reading the résumé. And even those hiring
managers who say they read a candidate's résumé first will almost
always go back and read the cover letter if the résumé sparks their
interest.

This means your cover letter ideally plays one of two roles: It can
serve as a preview to your résumé, enticing an employer to read
on, or it can function as a closing argument, enhancing the information presented in your résumé and making an employer want to
learn more.

In either case, a cover letter reveals things about your style and
personality that may clinch whether or not you get a call. Are you
assertive or subdued? Informed about the company or unaware of
its products? Try to make each cover letter personal; you should
rewrite your basic letter each time you apply for a job.

The Cold Call

When looking for a job,
don't neglect the "hidden
market." While it's easy to
pursue job openings that
you hear about either
through an ad or word of
mouth, you will likely be
one of hundreds of respon-
dents. By sending an unsolicited communication
requesting a meeting—
known as a cold call—to
firms likely to need someone with your experience,
you may uncover a hidden
opportunity or be first in
line when one emerges.

ASK THE EXPERTS

Do you always need to send a cover letter with your résumé?

There are a few situations where you might send your résumé without a cover letter, such as when you're submitting your résumé to a career database or filling out an application form on a company's Web site or when an employer has indicated "no cover letter necessary" (a rare occurrence). But in most cases, you do need to include one.

What a Cover Letter Should Do

■ Personally engage your reader

Wherever you can, mention the reader's name and/or company. Also mention the name of anyone the reader knows who helped you in your job search.

■ Indicate what you want

Are you applying for a job? Looking for an informational interview? Asking for industry contacts? Be clear about what you want.

■ Summarize your background

Don't rehash your résumé, but do give a brief summary of your qualifications—focusing on what you can contribute to that specific employer.

■ Reveal your personality

Managers generally end up hiring people they like, and a cover letter is your first opportunity to introduce yourself. Don't blow it by appearing pushy, insincere, or arrogant—make the reader want to meet you.

■ Initiate some response

Ideally, a cover letter should motivate the reader to take some action, such as call you for an interview or forward your résumé to a colleague. Keep the ball rolling by saying how you will follow up.

e-mail vs. print

The growing use of e-mail for job searches has had an even bigger effect on cover letters than it has on résumés. While the contents of a résumé have remained more or less the same, the cover letter has gotten the digital equivalent of a facelift.

These days, cover letters sent via e-mail tend to be much shorter and a bit more conversational than letters printed on heavy, ivory-colored paper. Sometimes referred to as a cover note or cover e-mail, a letter sent within an e-mail message is rarely more than three paragraphs—and often just a paragraph with a closing line.

The shorter length has to do with the way people read e-mail—in a hurry and looking at an area on a computer screen that is half the size of a regular sheet of paper. Plus, companies that solicit applications for open positions via e-mail tend to get inundated with responses, so they have less time to consider each applicant.

That doesn't mean you can send a cover e-mail that simply says, "Below, please find my résumé." It's still important to write an introduction to your résumé that showcases your personality and qualifications. With e-mail, you just have to state your case in much less space. In other words, keep it short. (For a sample cover e-mail, see page 145.)

E-mail Don'ts

■ Don't use all lowercase letters or take other digital shortcuts. Use proper capitalization, punctuation, and grammar.

■ Don't use formatting like bold or italics unless you are 100 percent sure the recipient's e-mail program can read it.

■ Don't use e-mail shorthand like abbreviations or **emoticons**—symbols such as the sideways happy face :-) used to indicate emotions.

■ If your e-mail program automatically adds a signature to messages (like your name and phone number), don't include a funny quote, political message, or other text that might be considered unprofessional.

■ Don't send your submission from your work e-mail address; it suggests that you regularly take care of personal business on company time.

FIRST PERSON DISASTER STORY

Cover Letter Malaise

I have been looking for a job for over nine months, and it seems like every résumé and cover letter I send out disappears without a response. At first I thought it was because my résumé wasn't any good, but I had some former colleagues look it over to make sure it was okay. Then I thought it had to be my cover letters, so I decided to stop sending them altogether. I figured that I could send out way more résumés that way, and hiring managers could cut right to the chase. But that was a big mistake. One day, when I called a company I was really interested in to follow up on my résumé, a person in HR told me that I wasn't considered for the job because I had chosen not to submit a cover letter. That job would've been perfect for me, so I quickly sent in one of my old standbys, but I guess it was too late. I haven't made that mistake again—now I send specific cover letters for every job, no matter what.

Jason L., Austin, Texas

the basic format

Some aspects of a cover letter will vary depending on whether it is sent by e-mail, on a printed page, or by fax, but the basic format is the same regardless of the distribution channel. The main difference is in the body or text of the letter: A printed page allows more room to expand. But even with print there should be no more than four to five paragraphs for your entire letter.

A Sender, recipient, date, and subject line

In an e-mail cover letter, this information appears in what is called the header—the fields that appear at the top of the message. An e-mail cover letter will also have a subject line, typically the title of the job you're applying for. For a printed cover letter, the placement of the sender's name and address, the date, and the recipient's name and address follow a particular format (for a sample, see page 145).

B Greeting

More formally known as a salutation, this is the word or phrase you use to address the recipient.

C Opening line

The first sentence lays out what you want and is often a separate paragraph. It should grab the reader's attention.

D Body of letter

In an e-mail, the body of your letter may be only one paragraph. With a printed cover letter, two to four paragraphs are acceptable.

E Closing

The closing is generally a separate line or two where you thank the recipient and promise or request some follow-up action.

F Signature

In a print cover letter, your signature typically appears below a word or phrase like "Sincerely," followed by a typed version of your name. In an e-mail cover note, you would also list your phone number after your typed-in name. (If you are not sending a résumé, all of your contact information should be included here also.)

Sample Cover Letter/E-mail

(A)

From: Ethan Sanders [esanders@webmail.net]

To: Madeline Lyons [madeline.lyons@printstuff.com]

Date: January 7, 2003

Subject: art director position

(B) Dear Ms. Lyons:

(C) I met your colleague Sam Greenberg at a Berkeley alumni event last week, and he mentioned that you are looking for an art director for your consumer publishing division.

(D) I recently moved back to the Bay Area after working for eight years at various publishing companies in New York and then as an art director at Raven Publishing. From what Sam told me, the position you are filling sounds like a great fit for my experience, so I have attached below a copy of my résumé for your consideration.

I will e-mail you next week to see if you have time for a brief phone call. Thank you for your time.

(E) Sincerely,

Ethan Sanders **(F)**
510-555-9789

choosing a greeting

Sometimes you need to do some sleuthing

Deciding what kind of greeting to use, particularly if you don't know the recipient's name, can be tricky.

Even when you are writing to a specific person, you may be uncertain whether "Dear Larry" is too familiar a greeting, or whether Pat Bain is a Mr. or Ms. Bain. When in doubt, the safest course of action is to use both a first and last name (as in "Dear Pat Bain"). You won't offend anyone by being too casual and you won't make a gender mistake.

What if you don't know the hiring manager's name?

Make an effort to find out who is screening résumés for an open position by calling the company and asking. (Sometimes a receptionist or assistant can be talked into revealing a contact name.) If you're sending your résumé without knowing whether there's an opening, you should definitely find someone in the appropriate department and address it to that person. A company's Web site is often a good source of information about the management team.

Dear Sales Manager

Dear Manager

Dear Sales Director

If you're applying for an opening in response to an ad that doesn't even give the company name, you may be able to figure it out with a little sleuthing. An e-mail address like "jobs@widgetsandtrinkets.com" usually means "www.widgetsandtrinkets.com" is the hiring company's Web site (though some job announcements give a recruiter's e-mail address instead).

ASK THE EXPERTS

I've been unable to track down the name of anyone to whom I should direct my submission. Is it okay to skip the greeting altogether?

In a cover letter sent by e-mail, this is an option, but the recipient may find it abrupt. For printed letters, skipping the greeting would certainly look strange. Instead, use a generic title that seems appropriate to the situation. For instance, if you are applying for a position as a sales associate, "Dear Sales Director," "Dear Sales Manager," or even just "Dear Manager" are all safe choices. "Dear Recruiter" is an option if you think a recruiter is screening candidates on behalf of the hiring company. Or, if you lack the information to be even that specific, you can start with a simple salutation like "Greetings" or "Hello." (For more casual industries or fields, "Hi" might be okay, but when in doubt, opt for the slightly more formal "Hello.")

Can I start with something really generic, like "To Whom It May Concern" or "Dear Sir or Madam"?

Starting a letter with "Dear Sirs" is a faux pas, but "Dear Sir or Madam" is also a bad choice. Why? It's not a commonly used greeting, so it sounds stuffy and old-fashioned—probably not the image you want to project. And "To Whom It May Concern" sounds like you're writing a letter to complain about poor customer service, which won't endear you to prospective employers. A simple salutation is preferable.

your opening line

Tell what you want— and what you can offer

The first line of your cover letter may be the most important one you'll write. Not unlike a pickup line in a social situation, it has to engage the other person right away—and a bad attempt can be an immediate turnoff, ruining anything else you have to say.

That's why it's important to consider your audience as you're writing: A research manager at an investment bank most likely has different expectations of job applicants than the head of a design department at an advertising agency. Tailor your opening to the industry and field you're in—and whenever possible, to the person you are addressing. (If a friend has given you a contact name, ask your friend for advice.)

No matter what approach you take, your first line should indicate what you want. In this age of information overload, you can't assume the recipient will read your whole letter. The first sentence is more likely to be read than anything else, so get to the point right away.

In that same carefully crafted opening line, you should also try to communicate what you can offer—which is very challenging and sometimes impossible to do without overwhelming the reader. The opposite page offers some examples that manage to express both what the writer wants and can contribute, all in one sentence.

Sample First Lines

- **Applying for a job? Explain how you learned about the opening.**

"Months of visiting your company's Web site to learn about job openings finally turned up the perfect position for me: an analyst in your audience research department."

"I was excited to see your advertisement in the *Boston Globe* for a paralegal in your trusts and estates practice."

- **Referred by a friend or colleague? Mention that person.**

"Karen Myers mentioned that you're looking for a new assistant at your veterinary clinic and suggested I get in touch."

"I met Julian Dobbs at a trade show sponsored by the Direct Marketing Association, and he thought my experience developing e-mail newsletters would be of interest to your colleagues in the marketing department."

- **Cold call? When writing an unsolicited letter to uncover a hidden opportunity (rather than responding to an ad or a tip about an opening), state what you want—and why you should get noticed—right off the bat.**

"After 15 years as a guidance counselor in the Westchester County school district, I am relocating to Boston this summer and looking for a new position at a high school in the area."

"My experience as a brand consultant for one of your competitors should warrant a look at my résumé to see whether my skills fit an opening at your firm."

filling out the middle

What goes into the middle of your cover letter will vary depending on multiple variables, like why you are writing, what you've said in your opening line, and how you're sending the letter (an e-mail cover letter should be much shorter).

In general, the body of your letter should elaborate on your first sentence, which should already have outlined what you want. If you're responding to an advertisement, describe how your experience matches the requirements listed for the position. (Some people even use bullet points to list each qualification, a sort of checklist that says, "I meet all the requirements for this job!") If you're writing a networking letter, give more background on how you got the recipient's name and then elaborate on your skills.

Like a résumé, a cover letter should focus on your achievements and accomplishments, not simply catalog where you have worked. Make the middle of your letter persuasive—whether you think of the letter as a sales pitch, a brochure, or an advertisement, your goal is to convince the reader you have something valuable to offer.

How long is too long?

For e-mail delivery, the body of your letter should be only one or two paragraphs; if you are mailing or faxing the letter, you can write up to five (but one or two may be enough). In any case, keep your paragraphs short: If a paragraph is more than six or seven lines on a page or the screen, it's too long.

Cover Letter Guidelines

■ **Don't rehash what's in your résumé.**
Summarize your background, but don't restate everything in your résumé. Your cover letter should give an overview—save the details for later.

■ **Show you know the company.**
Demonstrate you've done your homework by mentioning recent news about the employer—perhaps a strategy the company is pursuing or some development in the industry—then indicate how your skills can help.

■ **Mention a specific skill pertinent to the job.**
If you speak Spanish, lived in Beijing for two years, or used to be a fighter pilot, mention that in your cover letter—and explain how that skill is useful for the job you want.

■ **Say whether you're willing to relocate.**
If you're applying for a job in Tulsa and your return address is in Chicago, your letter should indicate you would be happy to move for the right job.

■ **Reference your education if it's impressive or relevant.**
If you just graduated from college and know the recipient of your letter went to the same school, or you recently got a degree necessary for a job opening, use your education to get a foot in the door.

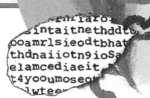

closing your letter

Mention your follow-up plan

Writing an ending for a cover letter is much easier than writing a beginning, because there is more of a consensus about how it should be done. Most career counselors advise job seekers to close a cover letter with two points:

1. thank the recipient for his or her time, and

2. indicate how you will follow up.

Expressing thanks is fairly straightforward: You can thank someone for looking at your résumé, giving you the opportunity to come in for an interview, or even offering you a job. Obviously, what you say will depend on your situation and what you are trying to accomplish with your letter.

Indicating how you will follow up can be trickier, especially if an employer's job advertisement requests, "No phone calls." The least assertive approach would be to say, "I hope to hear from you," but that leaves the ball in someone else's court. Unless a potential employer has banned follow-up calls, it's better to say you'll call in a few days to schedule a meeting or, if you have not gotten a response, to send another e-mail in a week or so.

Of course, sometimes you have little choice but to wait for the recipient to take action, such as when you are responding to an ad that does not list a company name, hiring manager, or phone number. In that case, "I look forward to hearing from you" is an acceptable last line.

Closing options

Sincerely,

Regards,

With regards,

Best,

Thank you,

Yours truly,

Sample Closing Statements

■ **Are you in contact with a specific person? Say how you'll follow up:**

"Do you have time for a brief conversation about whether my background fits any openings at your company? I'll call your office in a few days to follow up."

"Thank you for taking the time to look at my résumé. I'll e-mail you in a few days to arrange a time to talk on the phone."

■ **Responding to an ad that says "No phone calls"? Try to prompt a response:**

"I'll be in Los Angeles the week of May 15. Let me know if we can schedule an interview or meeting while I'm in town."

"I have some ideas about ways to make your expansion into Asia go smoothly based on my experience working in Hong Kong. Please e-mail or call me so we can arrange a time to talk."

style and tone

The style of your cover letter is not unlike the style of your outfit when you dress for an interview—you want to convey the right tone and attitude for the company you're applying to. But it's your cover letter that comes first and often determines whether you even get to show off that carefully selected interview attire.

If your writing style is overly formal or stuffy, the reader will assume you have the same manner in person (which may be fine for some companies, but probably not most). Similarly, if you are too casual or chatty, someone may think you aren't serious enough for the job.

The key is to find a middle ground that is appropriate for the job you want. Imagine you're having a conversation with a colleague—in a business meeting, not in a coffee lounge—and try to write in a style similar to how you would talk.

Once you have written a draft, read your letter out loud. Does it sound like you? Would you cringe if your friends read it? (The challenge is to express confidence without sounding arrogant or boastful.) As with your résumé, it's a good idea to have a friend or colleague read your letter before you send it out.

What to aim for	What to avoid
Sincere	Fawning
Natural	Unprofessional
Confident	Overbearing
Persuasive	Argumentative

Writing Tips

■ **Be concise.** Use short sentences to make your letter easy to read; long, run-on sentences are guaranteed to lose your audience.

■ **Don't start every sentence with "I."** Vary your sentence structure so that you don't come across as self-absorbed in your letter.

■ **Avoid conditional language.** Words like "perhaps," "might," and "could" make you seem timid or insecure.

■ **Use active, not passive, voice.** "I earned a promotion" is stronger than "I was awarded a promotion."

■ **Avoid exclamation points.** It's possible to express enthusiasm without tacking an exclamation point onto the end of a sentence. In a business letter, this punctuation mark comes across about as classy as a late-night TV infomercial.

■ **Use contractions sparingly.** A few contractions like "I'm" or "hasn't" are okay—and can keep you from sounding stiff—but too many can make your writing style seem unprofessional.

■ **Be careful with jargon.** Showing you know your field by using a few buzzwords is fine, but too many can suggest that you are unable to write to a general audience (and may overwhelm someone screening résumés for another department).

handling salary questions

One of the biggest dilemmas job seekers face is responding to advertisements that say, "Please include salary requirements."

Most career counselors recommend not revealing this information in a cover letter, for a number of reasons. You can price yourself out of consideration if your salary expectations are too high; if you come in too low, on the other hand, you can ruin your chance of being fairly compensated (or look like you don't have enough experience for the job). Whenever possible, it's best to save salary negotiations until after you have received an offer—or at least until you've had an interview and know more about the job.

That said, many people worry that if they don't indicate their salary requirements when this information is requested, they won't be considered for a job. Certainly this is a risk—some employers will only interview candidates they know they can afford. But most companies are savvy enough not to discount an otherwise good candidate for not "playing along," particularly if the salary question is handled tactfully.

The most common way to address the question without showing your hand is to give a salary range in your cover letter. Do some research first to make sure your range is in the ballpark for your industry or the company you are targeting. You can also say you would prefer to discuss salary requirements in an interview or that your salary needs depend on the total compensation package (salary plus benefits, stock options, and bonuses).

ASK THE EXPERTS

Most places where I'm applying ask for salary requirements. I was well paid at my last post, and I don't want to price myself out of consideration. Any suggestions?

If you want room to maneuver, try giving a range, describing your compensation as having been "between $70,000 and $85,000 in the past five years," and say that you're hoping to stay at the top of that range, including bonuses. Of course, if that's too specific, reference industry figures: "My research indicates similar jobs in the industry pay between $45,000 and $60,000. If your company is in this range, I'm sure we can agree on a fair salary."

I'd much prefer to discuss salary in person. How can I avoid naming a number without putting off prospective employers?

Defer the discussion in a professional manner in your cover letter: "My salary requirements are flexible and negotiable. I will be happy to discuss specifics in an interview."

Are there any times when it is advisable to provide a salary requirement?

When working with a recruiter, job seekers are expected to reveal their salary requirements. (A recruiter needs to know what you expect to earn in order to market you appropriately.) Even if you do not feel comfortable putting salary data in a letter to a recruiter, be prepared to discuss it in person or over the phone.

do gimmicks work?

Unconventional approaches can be risky

Hiring managers and career counselors express mixed feelings about cover letters that rely on gimmicks—attention-getting ploys to make a cover letter stand out. Examples might be writing your cover letter in the form of a TV script (say, when applying for a job with a television show) or delivering your letter and résumé with a jar of salsa (to drive home the message that you have ideas for "spicing up" the company's marketing efforts).

Do these offbeat strategies work? Unfortunately, there's no clear answer. The best advice may be: Proceed with caution. When surveyed, human resources managers offered contradictory opinions. Some gave anecdotes about gimmicks that won them over, while others claimed such ploys were always a turnoff.

When in doubt, take a cue from the industry you work in, and do your homework on the company or person you are targeting. The director of security at a casino may not be amused by a cover letter that arrives in the form of a ransom note, but the head of creative services at an advertising agency may be open to an unconventional approach.

Over-the-Top Opener

To Whom It May Concern:

Stop playing hard to get! Your company has been running the same ad for the same editorial assistant position for the past few months, and yet somehow you've managed to overlook my résumé along with those of some other really qualified people. Despite your poor judgment, I'm going to cut you some slack. I've decided to start working for you full-time. We'll figure out my salary later.

Yes, I know this is somewhat abrupt, but we need each other. I'm sure you'll see that I'm right for the job once I've started. I'm creative, I've got lots of initiative, and I've got all the experience you have been talking about in your job description. I've attached my résumé to this letter just to refresh your memory, but I'm sure you'll see that this is the perfect solution once I start on Monday. Call me.

On-the-Mark Opener

Dear Mr. Thomas:

As a longtime reader of *Adventure Travel* magazine, I was excited to see your advertisement in the *New York Times* for an editorial assistant.

As you will see from the enclosed résumé, I graduated at the top of my class this past May. Since then I've been putting my journalism degree and leadership experience to good use as an intern at *Travel Agent* magazine. As specified in your ad, I am proficient in Microsoft Word and QuarkXPress and am willing to travel. I would really appreciate the opportunity to discuss your editorial needs. I will plan on calling you Monday afternoon to see if we can set up an appointment.

now what do I do?

Answers to common questions

Where can I find background information about a company online?

A good place to start is the company's Web site. Look for links that say something like "company information" or "about us." Most companies post recent news, information about the management team, and sometimes a list of clients. Other good sources for company news and data are Hoover's Online (**www.hoovers.com**) and PR Newswire (**www.prnewswire.com**). For feedback from current or former employees about the company's culture, try Vault (**www.vault.com**), a career Web site that has message boards dedicated to specific companies.

How can I research salary data?

Trade associations often publish salary information for specific industries, based on surveys of association members. **Salary.com** and many career Web sites also offer tools that let visitors search for salary data according to industry, job title, and geographic area. Another way to research the market is to look at classified ads for your field, some of which list pay ranges.

Should I mention in my cover letter that I'm pregnant?

It's best not to mention a pregnancy when you send a cover letter and résumé, since employers might be hesitant to hire someone who will need time off shortly after starting a new job. If your pregnancy is obvious, the topic will come up in an interview. If it's not, gauge the situation before deciding when and how to bring it up.

Should I include information about personal interests or hobbies in my cover letter?

Generally, no. Focus on your professional qualifications and save your extracurricular interests for the "getting to know you" phase of an interview. One exception would be a hobby that relates to the job you want. If you are applying for a marketing job with the NBA, it would be appropriate to demonstrate your enthusiasm for the game by mentioning your Tuesday night basketball club.

Is it ever okay to send a cover letter that's more than one page?

The situations that would warrant a longer cover letter are rare—perhaps for some upper-level management positions or overseas jobs. You should generally stick to one page, and less if you are using e-mail.

As I sit down to write my first cover letter, are there any opening lines that I should avoid?

Stay away from phrases that are used over and over in cover letters, such as "Enclosed please find my résumé," or "I am writing to apply for the position you advertised." While there's nothing inherently wrong with these statements, any cover letter that starts this way sounds like dozens of other letters a hiring manager has already seen. Your goal is to distinguish yourself from the rest of the pack—not to follow the herd.

Now where do I go?

WEB SITES

www.hoovers.com
Profiles, news, and data for thousands of companies.

www.prnewswire.com
Corporate press releases and news.

www.vault.com
Career advice and feedback on specific companies.

www.salary.com
Tools to find salary data.

BOOKS

Cover Letters for Dummies
by Joyce Lain Kennedy
General guidelines for writing cover letters.

For pointers on e-mail etiquette:

E Writing: 21st Century Tools for Effective Communication
by Dianna Booher

The Elements of E-Mail Style: Communicate Effectively Via Electronic Mail
by David Angell and Brent Heslop

Types of cover letters

the cover e-mail

The most important thing to keep in mind when writing a cover letter in an e-mail message is to keep it brief. People read e-mail much more quickly than they do print text and rarely have the patience to scroll through page after page on a computer screen.

Formatting tips

Choosing a subject

Be specific with your subject line. Give the exact title of the job you are applying for; don't just type "position you advertised." If a friend or colleague has given you a contact name, indicate that in the subject line, e.g., "Referred by Jay Wong."

Where to put your contact info

When pasting your résumé into an e-mail message, make sure all of your contact information appears within your résumé (including your name, phone number, mailing address, and e-mail address). You don't need to repeat this information below your signature, but you might want to include your phone number twice (once in the résumé section and once below your signature in the cover letter section). If you are not sending a résumé, include your contact information after your name.

How to paste in your résumé

Be sure your résumé has been saved as plain text (see page 109) before pasting it into your e-mail message. You may want to use some kind of dividing line between your signature and the beginning of your résumé.

Sample Cover E-mail

From: Monica Salinas [msalinas@webmail.net]
Date: Wed 2/5/03 11:35 AM

To: areynolds@theevergreenstore.com

Subject: store manager position at the Evergreen

Dear Ann Reynolds,

I've been poring over the classifieds for weeks looking for just the type of retail management position you advertised in *The Oregonian* on Sunday.

My three years of experience as an associate manager at Nelson's, a specialty clothing store, contributed to annual sales increases of 10 to 15 percent. Now I'd like to transfer that experience to a store with a product line like yours that matches my environmental interests. (I was an environmental studies major at Portland State University and spent two years after college working for Greenpeace.)

My résumé is pasted below. I'll call you next week to see if we can set up a time to talk.

Sincerely,

Monica Salinas
503-555-6941

printed letters

Follow the formal business letter format

Print cover letters are less common in this age of electronic communication, but they do still exist. Here are a few guidelines for formatting your cover letter if you are sending it via old-fashioned postal mail—or by fax.

A Your Address

For a print letter, your address is typically centered at the top of the page. For consistency, it should appear the same way it does on your résumé (i.e., don't list your e-mail address above your phone number on your résumé and then do the opposite on your cover letter).

B The Date

Type the full date on the left side of the page. Leave a line or two of space between the date and the recipient's address below.

C Recipient and Greeting

Include the recipient's full address—and perhaps a phone number (this way, when you make a copy of the letter for your records, you'll also have the phone number on file). Then skip a line and type your greeting (for more on greetings, see page 126).

D Body of Letter

In typical business writing style, each paragraph is aligned flush left (i.e., don't indent), with a blank line between paragraphs. (For more on what to say, see Chapter 6.)

E Your Signature

After your last paragraph, leave a line or two of space and then type a closing (see page 132), followed by several blank lines, then a typed version of your name. Don't forget to sign the letter before you send it!

Sample Print Cover Letter

A

Jerome Dawanda
112 Elm Avenue, #8F
Brooklyn, NY 54321
jdawanda@webmail.net
718-555-8750

B May 30, 2003

Alvin Newman
The Newman Gallery
319 W. 23rd Street
New York, NY 10011

C Dear Mr. Newman:

It was nice meeting you at the Met yesterday. As I mentioned, I've been a fan of your gallery since my dad first brought me there when I was barely tall enough to see the photographs.

D Enclosed is a copy of my résumé, as you requested. Spring semester ends in mid-May, so I am available anytime after that for a summer internship. I've been volunteering at the International Photography Gallery in Midtown this year, primarily doing research for an upcoming exhibit about digital photography.

I would love to show you my portfolio and talk more about the project we discussed. I will call you next week to see when would be a good time for me to stop by. Thank you for your time.

Sincerely,

Jerome Dawanda **E**

Jerome Dawanda

responding to an ad

Writing in response to a job advertisement can be the easiest letter to write because you have more information to work with. Since most employers list certain qualifications necessary for a particular position—e.g., "a bachelor's degree in communications" or "five years of experience handling public relations for an entertainment company"—you generally know what the employer wants.

Your cover letter should first identify what position you are applying for and where you saw the opening advertised. Companies pay to advertise available jobs, so they like to know which sources turn up the best candidates. How you found out about the job also tells the employer something about your background. For example, if you saw an ad in a particular trade publication, it indicates that you keep up with industry developments.

The body of your letter or e-mail should highlight your qualifications, using the employer's job requirements as a guide. For instance, if a job listing says a certain type of experience or degree is "required," you should list that before something that is "preferred." Some career counselors advise using a list format for your qualifications (see example on the opposite page), but you can also do it in a paragraph of text.

In your closing, don't forget to thank the recipient and indicate how you will follow up. For advice on what to do if you don't know who the recipient is—e.g., you have only a cryptic e-mail address—see page 126.

Ruth Orlins
24 Grove Avenue
Honolulu, HI 23456
845-555-1295

April 20, 2003

Carol Whitley
General Manager
Yardley Hotel
2000 Palm Court Drive
Key West, FL 12345

Dear Ms. Whitley:

The Concierge position you advertised on the *Resort Hospitality* Web site is a perfect match for my qualifications.

Your job requirements specify six-plus years' experience as a concierge at a major resort hotel. I have eight years' experience, including six at my present job as concierge of the Hillside Regency Waikiki Resort & Spa, a 1,200+ room vacation resort in Honolulu, Hawaii.

Your job requires:	I possess:
Regional Knowledge	Firsthand knowledge of restaurants, activities (scuba diving, windsurfing, golfing), and sights around the Keys, gained while growing up in the area and during two years as concierge at Four Palms resort in Key West, Florida.
Hospitality Management Education	Bachelor's degree in Hospitality Management from Rutgers University
Guest Service Expertise	Excellent references that attest to my skills dealing with a wide range of guests, as well as nine commendations for providing exemplary service.

A copy of my résumé is enclosed. I will e-mail you next week to see whether you would like to set up a time to talk.

Best,

Ruth Orlins

Ruth Orlins

the networking letter

A networking cover letter is any letter you write to people within your network of contacts—a friend, a relative, a business colleague, a former classmate, or other acquaintances in your industry. Since most people find out about job openings through networking—not through classified ads or company job postings—this is a key aspect of any job search.

The most important thing to remember is that networking is primarily about asking for advice or information—not blatantly asking someone to give you a job.

What is a networking letter for?

- To let people know you're looking for work.
- To learn about job openings at the recipient's company.
- To get background information for an interview.
- To find out about openings at other companies.
- To get names of other people to contact.

How should it be structured?

- Say who referred you.
- Indicate why you are writing (i.e., be as clear as possible about what you want).
- Give a brief summary of your qualifications.
- Thank the recipient and say how you'll follow up.

Don't forget to thank your contacts

Be sure to send a thank-you note (see page 156) to anyone who helps you during your job search—immediately after they do you a favor and then again to let them know how things worked out (especially once you have found a job).

ⒶSK THE EXPERTS

Is it better to call or to write?

These days, many people prefer to be contacted by e-mail rather than interrupted by a phone call. The advantage of e-mail is that the recipient can read it when she has time; the disadvantage is it might get lost in the shuffle. A good strategy is to send an e-mail first, especially to someone you don't know, and then follow up a few days later with a phone call. Sending a printed letter is another option—while slower, some potential employers may prefer a formal package over an e-mail.

Is it okay to use the name of the person who referred me?

In most cases, yes, but it's always a good idea to ask first—e.g., if a college classmate gives you a list of three people to contact, be sure to ask if it's okay for you to use his or her name when you write or call. (It's also helpful to ask whether each contact person prefers e-mail or the phone.)

FIRST PERSON SUCCESS STORY

Net Worth

After I was laid off from my job as a copywriter at an advertising agency, I thought it would be a good idea to do some networking at an advertising conference that happened to be taking place nearby. At first, I was uncomfortable telling anyone I was looking for a job, but I finally got up the nerve to ask some people whether they knew of any companies that were hiring. One woman gave me the name of a coworker at her agency who she said might be looking to hire someone. She sounded kind of doubtful, so I wasn't optimistic, but I decided to send him an e-mail anyway. It took weeks to close the deal, but that e-mail finally led to a job offer! I know everybody says the best way to find a job is through networking—and now I'm a firm believer in that advice.

—Mark A., Oakland, California

the cold call

In sales, the term **cold call** refers to contact made with a customer who has not indicated any interest in the product being sold; in a job search, the term describes roughly the same scenario. The cold call letter, sometimes called a **broadcast letter**, is used when you have no idea whether a company has an open position that suits your qualifications—you're targeting the company because you're interested in what it does.

For instance, if you are a project manager who was recently laid off from a software company, you might contact other technology companies in the area to see whether they have any jobs available (or want to meet with you in case they will be hiring in the future). Your best strategy is to do your homework and find companies that might be interested in someone with your skills—not to simply write every member of the local Chamber of Commerce.

It's also better to get in touch with someone in the department you want to work in—writing to a specific person, if possible—than to send a generic letter to human resources. (The human resources department might not know about jobs available in various departments and may even discard your résumé if no immediate opening is on the horizon.) Someone from the department is more likely to meet with you if you sound interesting to them. It's also okay to contact more than one person at a company, but if you get a response, be sure to mention anyone else you've contacted.

How to get names

The Web is a great tool for this type of research. On many company Web sites you'll find company news, management bios, and other information that might reveal who manages a particular department. You can usually get at least a phone number from the Web site and call the company to find out who is, say, head of sales.

Cold Call Letter

First, say why you're writing.

Then, briefly summarize your background and skills—and show what you can contribute to the company.

Finally, thank the recipient for his or her time and say how you'll follow up.

Dear Ms. Gamine:

I am a first-year law student at New York University, and I am writing to find out whether you will be hiring any summer associates this year.

Prior to law school, I spent two years as a paralegal in Brown, Smith & Wiley's intellectual property practice, and I am planning to specialize in patent law after I graduate. I recently wrote an article about the United States Patent and Trademark Office's Web site for *Law Practice* magazine, and I am particularly interested in how technology has changed how patents are issued.

Thank you for taking the time to look at my résumé, which is pasted below. I will call you next week to see whether you have time for a brief phone call.

Sincerely,

Susan Marshall

212-555-8768

contacting a recruiter

Describe your qualifications and interests

There are two reasons to contact **recruiters**—professionals who work with companies to fill positions—during your job search: because you applied for a position a recruiter is filling or you want to work with a recruiting firm to find out about job openings.

In the first case, the letter you send will be like any other cover letter you write to apply for a job (in fact, when replying to some job advertisements you may be writing to a recruiter, also known as a headhunter, without realizing it). If, on the other hand, you are approaching recruiters to see whether they'll consider you for any open positions with their clients, the letter you write will be somewhat different.

In that case, it's generally a good idea to call the firm first—to find out whether it's an agency you want to work with, what industry or field they focus on, and how you should submit your résumé. Keep in mind that some recruiters might tell you that your experience does not fit the types of positions they fill, and others might not take or return your phone call. Recruiters are in business to find good candidates for their clients, not to help you find work.

When writing to a recruiter, you should emphasize your qualifications and interests, since you are not targeting a specific company. Describe what type of position you want, indicate whether you are willing to relocate, and say you will call in a few days to follow up. It's also more common to indicate your salary requirements when contacting a recruiter than an employer (see page 137), though you may want to save that discussion for a phone call.

ASK THE EXPERTS

Is it okay to tell a recruiter not to contact me at the office?

Either in your cover letter or on the phone—or both—you should be clear about the best way to contact you. If your job search is confidential, be sure to mention that (and don't give your office phone number), but you also need to make yourself accessible so a recruiter can reach you during business hours (e.g., give your cell phone number or set up a personal e-mail address you can check from work).

Can I ask a recruiter not to submit my résumé to a company without my permission?

Absolutely. If a headhunter balks at that request, it's probably not someone you want to work with.

Should I tell a recruiter why I'm looking for work?

Depending on your situation, your cover letter may not be the best place to address the topic, since you have less room to explain yourself. For instance, if you write and say you were just laid off, it might raise questions in the recruiter's mind about why you lost your job—better to explain the situation in person. If, on the other hand, you are still employed and looking for work, say, with a smaller company, that is something you might safely mention in your letter.

Do I have to pay the recruiter?

In most cases, no. Recruiters typically get paid by the company filling a position, either through a retainer or a commission—usually some percentage of the annual salary. (The payment is not deducted from the employee's salary; that's just the figure used to determine the recruiter's commission.) In rare cases, a recruiter may ask a job seeker for payment—in which case, find another headhunter.

thank-you notes

Express your appreciation

Thank-you notes are an important part of the job search. What you say depends on the circumstances but, regardless of the occasion, you should aim to keep it short.

If you are thanking someone for an interview, it's okay to mention a thing or two that came up in your meeting (or something you forgot to bring up), but beware of weighing down what's meant to be an expression of gratitude with any overly blatant self-promotion.

Opt for e-mail if time is of the essence or you want to start a dialogue (it's easier for the recipient to respond). There are, however, occasions when a handwritten note is more appropriate, such as after you've accepted a job offer or when someone has really helped you out.

From: Allen Marks [amarks@webmail.net]   Date: Wed 2/18/03 2:12 PM

To: bwalker@walkerbroker.com

Subject: Thanks for your help

Bill,

Thank you for taking the time to meet with me yesterday and for putting me in touch with your friend at Cook Investments. I sent Paul a note this morning. I will let you know how that works out.

Your advice about investigating small brokerage firms makes sense, so I'm going to see what I can find out about that market. Good luck with your conference next week, and thanks again for your help.

Regards,

Allen

When to Send a Thank-You Note

■ **After an interview**
Feel free to reiterate something you mentioned in the interview, but don't go overboard. Send a thank-you even if you feel the interview didn't go well; it shows you are professional and leaves the door open for a follow-up discussion.

■ **After someone has done you a favor**
If someone forwarded your résumé to a colleague, gave you contact names, or wrote a nice reference for you, a thank-you note is in order.

■ **After receiving and accepting a job offer**
Send a quick e-mail reiterating how much you look forward to working for the company.

■ **After being turned down**
Even if you didn't get a job, send a thank-you note. The person hired might not work out or there may be other openings at the company. A thank-you note will strengthen the good impression you have made and underscore your interest in the company.

■ **After starting a new job**
Send a note to everybody in your network letting them know where you landed and thanking them for their help.

now what do I do?

Answers to common questions

Should I send a thank-you note to everyone I met during an interview or just the hiring manager?

Use your judgment. If you spent most of your time with two people and briefly met three others, it's okay to thank just the two who seem to be responsible for making the hiring decision. In some cases, you might need to send only one thank-you note.

I'm applying for another job at my company but don't want my boss to know. Should I indicate that in my cover letter?

It would be better to communicate that in person; if you put it in a letter, you never know where that piece of paper—or e-mail—is going to end up. See if you can talk to the hiring manager, or ask for advice from someone in human resources, about keeping your application confidential.

If I send a networking e-mail and don't hear back, how soon should I follow up?

It depends on the circumstances. Waiting a week to give someone a chance to write or call back is a good rule of thumb. But if you're in a time-sensitive situation, three or four days might be appropriate.

What if I don't get a response after sending two e-mail messages?

Try sending another message—or, if it seems appropriate, calling. But if you haven't heard back after three attempts, it may be time to move on.

I'm sending out several networking letters. Should I include résumés with them?

It depends on the situation. If you know there's an open position at the recipient's company, then sending a résumé is not inappropriate. Similarly, if someone you met at a cocktail party asked you to send a résumé, obviously you should. When in doubt, leave it out of your initial contact and ask if it's okay to send one. (If you don't hear back, send a follow-up e-mail with a résumé a few days later; the worst that can happen is it gets ignored.)

I'm interested in working for a company that does not list any names of employees on its Web site. How do I find out the right person to contact about a job?

You can try calling the company and asking who manages a particular department. If the receptionist is unwilling to give out that information, call back and ask for a specific department, then see if the person you are transferred to is more forthcoming. If all else fails, call back and ask for human resources, then ask who handles recruiting for that department. This may not land your résumé directly with the department you are targeting, but at least you'll be only one step away.

Now where do I go?

WEB SITES

Recruiters Online Network
www.ipa.com
Good place to search for recruiting firms, organized by specialty and location.

Association of Executive Search Consultants
www.aesc.org
Lists member executive search firms.

CareerCity
www.careercity.com
Offers articles on writing cover letters.

BOOKS

175 High-Impact Cover Letters, 3rd Edition
by Richard H. Beatty

101 Best Cover Letters
by Jay A. Block and Michael Betrus

Winning Cover Letters
by Robin Ryan

Sending it out

Make sure nothing you've said—
or haven't said—will eliminate
you from consideration.

one last look

Once you think your résumé and cover letter are ready to go, take a step back and think again. As tempting as it may be to pop them in the mail or hit that Send button, you don't want to cut corners at the end.

Give yourself a fresh perspective by taking a break for an hour or two—or sleep on it and take another look in the morning. When you're ready to give your cover letter and résumé a final pass, use the checklist on the opposite page to make sure you are presenting yourself in the best possible light.

Then, if you haven't done so already, send a copy of your résumé and cover letter to a colleague or a friend and ask for feedback. Even if you got a second opinion on an earlier draft, you should still have someone check your final version to make sure no glaring errors or incomprehensible phrases have sneaked in.

Once you're satisfied with the final version, use the tips in this chapter to make sure there are no problems between hitting the Send button and an employer opening your document on the other end. Especially if you're sending an electronic version of your résumé, there are a lot of computer quirks you'll need to look out for so all your hard work creating these documents doesn't get ruined by a transmission error.

Résumé & Cover Letter Checklist

■ **Is it clear what you want to do next?**
You may know what you want to do, but if your cover letter and résumé don't make that clear, employers won't know what to do with you—so they won't call.

■ **Do your cover letter and résumé work together?**
Make sure your cover letter and résumé are sending the same message. If one says you're a marketing ace and the other focuses on your sales experience, employers will think you lack direction.

■ **Do you talk about what you achieved—or just what you did?**
If you've only described how you spent your days in various positions, you need to go back and fill in more about your accomplishments—how your employer benefited from having you on staff.

■ **Are your cover letter and résumé interesting?**
Dull documents suggest a dull job candidate. If yours read like instruction manuals, they'll end up in the dusty pile on the farthest corner of someone's desk.

■ **Will anything in your résumé or cover letter raise a red flag?**
Make sure nothing you've said—or haven't said—will eliminate you from consideration for a position. (See Chapter 4 for more on handling résumé challenges.)

■ **Are you putting your best foot forward?**
When it comes to writing a cover letter and résumé, your most impressive qualifications should always be at the top of the page. You never know whether your reader will make it to the end.

■ **Did you proofread your documents?**
Last, but certainly not least, make sure you've eliminated any misspellings or grammatical errors. Many employers will disqualify a candidate from consideration simply due to a typo; don't rule yourself out by mixing up "there" and "their."

printing and mailing

Some employers will ask you to send a résumé the old-fashioned way: through the mail (some managers prefer to deal with paper; others don't want to give out their e-mail address for fear they'll be inundated with follow-up messages). If that's the case, best not to buck the system. When you're asked to go postal, follow the guidelines below, which may have faded from memory with the dawning of the digital age.

ASK THE EXPERTS

Is it okay to handwrite the addresses on the envelope when I'm mailing my résumé, or should I print out labels?

Most employers probably won't frown on a handwritten address, but it's certainly preferable to print address labels from your computer if you can. Use the Help function in Microsoft Word to get directions on printing labels; in a pinch, you can also print addresses on regular paper, then glue or tape that paper to your envelope. But if the envelope ends up looking like a grade school art project, you're better off writing the address by hand.

I don't have a good printer at home. Is it okay to print one copy of my résumé on a friend's printer and then make additional photocopies to send?

That's a bad option for two reasons: One, it doesn't allow you to revise your résumé for different job openings, and two, the quality of a photocopy is never as good as the version that comes off the printer. Don't skimp on details like print quality—it will suggest you're likely to take shortcuts on the job as well.

Is it better to send my résumé with an overnight service or by regular mail?

The advantage of using an overnight delivery service is that you can make sure your envelope was received—and if you're applying for a job close to the deadline, it's worth paying for overnight service. But it's an expensive alternative to regular mail and, in the eyes of some employers, you may look like you have money to burn—not necessarily a good thing. Use it only when necessary, or go with a less expensive option, like second-day delivery.

When You're Ready to Print

■ Use high-quality white or off-white paper, which is easy to read and makes better photocopies than colored paper or shades of gray.

■ Print on only one side of the page—saving trees is a noble goal, but you can't be sure employers will look on the back of your résumé.

■ Whenever possible, use a laser printer to print your cover letter and résumé. If you use an inkjet printer, make sure the ink won't run if the page gets wet.

■ Check that your contact information is on each page of your résumé and cover letter. But don't staple the pages together—someone will have to remove the staple to make copies.

Mailing Tips

If you really want to make a good impression, don't fold your résumé in thirds and stuff it into a letter-size envelope—use one the size of the page. You'll have to pay additional postage to send it, but employers won't have to fiddle with creased pages. (It also makes photocopying easier.)

pasting and e-mailing

Sending your résumé within an e-mail message

There are two ways you can send your résumé by e-mail: either pasted into the body of a message or as an attachment—a separate file that is electronically paper clipped to your outgoing message.

Most employers prefer to receive résumés that are pasted into an e-mail message because it's quicker for them to scan and it avoids potential problems such as catching a computer virus. Some job advertisements will stipulate "no attachments," in which case you should send your documents within your e-mail message.

Otherwise, it's okay to send your résumé both ways: within the message and also as an attachment. If you take this route, note in your cover letter that you have also enclosed your résumé as an attached file.

If you have already saved a version of your résumé and cover letter in plain text (see page 109), you're halfway through the process of transferring your documents into an e-mail message. But there is an additional step you need to take before hitting the Send button. Since various e-mail programs have different limits on the number of characters that can fit on each line of an e-mail message, your text will have awkward line breaks if your line limit is higher than your recipient's. That's why it's advisable to adjust the number of characters on each line of your document to 65 or less—including spaces—before pasting it into an e-mail message. (See opposite page for directions.) You will also need a clear and concise subject line (e.g., the name of the person who referred you, or the title of the position advertised).

Sample e-mail showing résumé within the e-mail and attached.

166

STEP BY STEP

Copying Your Cover Letter and Résumé into an E-mail

1. Open the version of your résumé and cover letter you have saved as plain text. To make things easier, cut and paste your cover letter and résumé into one file and save them (as text only) under a new name.

2. With your new document open, highlight a line of text (choose the one that reaches farthest toward the right margin), then select Tools and Word Count. A new window will open that lists several numbers, including one that says "Characters (with spaces)"—that number will probably be higher than 100, but your goal is to make it 65 or less. Click the Close button in that window.

3. Adjust the right margin of your document so your lines are shorter and check the word count again. Keep moving the margin boundary until the word count for the longest line on the page is 65 characters or less (with spaces). (For more on adjusting margins, see page 107.)

4. Once you have reached that goal, select File, then Save As. A new window will open. At the bottom of the window, where it says "Save as Type," click the little arrow on the right, then select "Text only with line breaks." Click the Save button.

5. You'll have to close your document and reopen it before copying and pasting the contents into a new e-mail message. With your document open, choose Edit, then Select All, then Edit and Copy. Open a new e-mail message and paste the text you copied into the message.

6. Before you click the Send button, double-check the text to make sure you have replaced bullets with asterisks, used capital letters for headers, and have not repeated your contact information in your cover letter and résumé. It's also a good idea to send a test version to yourself before sending it to an employer.

attaching a file

Employers often say they prefer to receive résumés within an e-mail message, but some job listings do indicate it's okay to send your résumé as an attachment, a file electronically clipped to your e-mail. It's fine to do both, unless the listing states that the company does not want attachments.

When sending your résumé as an attached file, you should still write or paste your cover letter into the body of an e-mail message. (Yes, you do need to write a formal cover letter; don't just send an e-mail message saying, "I'd like to apply for the sales position you advertised. Attached is my résumé.") Be sure to include your contact information below your signature in your e-mail message as well as on your résumé.

If you are sending an attachment, give the file a name that is descriptive. Call it Résumé and you can bet the recipient will have received dozens or even hundreds of other attachments with the same name—and have trouble keeping track of yours. A good option is to call your file something that incorporates your first initial and last name, like JKellerResume.

Finally, be sure to remember to attach the file. It's not uncommon for even savvy Internet users to type the text of an e-mail message, indicate they have attached a file, and then forget to go through the process of attaching it. Don't get distracted—you'll make a poor first impression if you have to resend your e-mail with a note saying, "I forgot to add the attachment in my last message."

STEP BY STEP

Attaching a Document to an E-mail Message

1. First, open your résumé and make sure it is ready to be sent. If necessary, save it with a distinctive name. It's okay to save it as a regular Microsoft Word document, with formatting, as long as you are sending a plain text version of your résumé within your e-mail message. If you're not including it in the body of your e-mail, you should consider saving it as a text-only file (see page 109) to be sure the recipient can read it.

2. Close your résumé and open a new e-mail message. Once you have typed (or pasted) your cover letter into the body of the e-mail message, follow your e-mail software program's instructions for attaching your résumé to your message. (Using Microsoft Outlook, select Insert, then File, to add an attachment, or click the paper clip icon in the toolbar. For other e-mail programs, use the Help feature if you need instructions on sending attachments.)

3. You may have to click through several folders on your computer to find the file you want to attach. Also, it's best to close the file before sending; most computers won't send a file if it's open. Once you have selected the résumé you want to send, click Insert (or OK, depending on the program you're using). Be sure you see an icon or the name of the file you have attached somewhere within your message before you click Send!

online forms

Submitting a résumé via an **online application form** usually occurs in one of two cases: applying for a job at a company's Web site or submitting a résumé to a recruiting Web site so it can be viewed by many different employers.

In either case, the process typically involves filling out the electronic version of an application form as well as copying and pasting a traditional résumé as a single file (though some sites will let you do both). (The application forms are also known as **résumé builders**, since they use information from your résumé and ask you to build upon it in their application forms.)

Although some of the questions these online forms ask are the same from site to site—your name, address, and phone number, for starters—each site has its own process, so unfortunately you'll probably find yourself typing the same information many times. To speed up the process, some job seekers prefer to cut and paste sections of their résumé in response to specific questions (like, "What is your objective?").

One advantage of the cut-and-paste approach is that you can use text you've already run through spell check; a hazard of typing everything from scratch is that you may make some mistakes. Most of these sites allow you to preview your online form as you go through the process of entering your information, so be sure to proofread the preview screen carefully and fix any errors.

What's your title?

Many résumé builders ask you to write a title or headline for your résumé. Pick something descriptive and catchy (i.e., Technical Sales Representative, C/C++ Software Developer); it will be the first thing employers see when searching for job candidates. Also, include plenty of keywords—terms or phrases employers are likely to search for—as you enter your information (see page 112). A résumé packed with keywords is more likely to be read—and to land an interview.

ASK THE EXPERTS

Do I have to answer all the questions these online forms ask?

Some Web forms require users to fill in every field—meaning you can't skip any questions—while others indicate which fields must be filled in and which are optional. If there's something you really don't want to answer, sometimes typing any text, like "not applicable" or "will discuss," will satisfy the software program and let you move on.

What if I don't finish entering my résumé in one sitting?

Most sites will let you save your work and come back to finish it later. Your résumé won't be added to the database until you complete the process, so don't worry—employers won't be able to access your résumé until it's finished.

Once I submit my résumé, who else has access to this database?

Policies vary, but most sites require employers to sign up—and usually pay a fee—before they can search the résumé database. If you'd prefer to keep your job search confidential, see page 176 for tips.

Can I delete my résumé if I decide I no longer want it in the database?

Most recruiting Web sites let you delete your résumé or, in some cases, just "hide" it so no one will have access to it when you're no longer looking for a job. (This option allows you to revise your résumé and repost it without retyping all your data if you enter the job market two years down the road.)

sample résumé builder

Many companies prefer online submissions

NAME

Prefix: Mr. ⬍

First Name: Jason   Middle Name: S.

Last Name: Lassero   Suffix: Jr ⬍

CONTACT INFO

Address: Home ⬍   Phone: 504-555-1602

Street: 115 Tennyson St.   E-mail: Jlassero@lassero.com

City: Metairie   State: Louisiana ⬍

Postal Code: 12345   Province/County: Kings Parish

Country: United States ⬍

EMPLOYMENT

Most Recent Employer: Dixie Beverage Co.

Title: Production Supervisor

Job Description: Plant Management

Are you willing to relocate? ⦿ Yes ◯ No

Are you willing to travel? ⦿ Yes ◯ No

What percentage are you willing to travel? 10

Where heard? Times Picayune advertisement

Ad Code: ZZYZ123

What countries are you legally authorized to work in?

United States ⦿ Yes ◯ No

United Kingdom ◯ Yes ⦿ No

EDUCATION

School (Do not abbreviate): Louisiana State University

Education Level Attained: Bachelor of Science ⬍

Major/Subject: Mechanical Engineering

GPA: 3.6   Grad Date 05 / 97 (MM/YY)

SKILLS AND PREFERENCES

Job Type Preference: | Production Director | ⬍ |

Job Type Preference 2: | Production Supervisor | ⬍ |

Geographical Preference: | Southeast | ⬍ |

Geographical Preference 2: | Southwest |

Technical Skills: (512 character max)

Six Sigma quality program proficiency.
Familiarity with wide range of production
control software.

Non-technical Skills: (512 character max)

Capable team leader.
Innovative, resourceful manager.
Experienced at cost control and budget
management.

Career Objectives: (2000 character max)

To find a production management position
that fully utilizes my skills and experience.

RESUME

Resume: (1600 character max)

Summary of Qualifications
*Engineer and manager with five years production and operations experience
*Proven track record of increasing productivity and quality control through implementa-
tion of employee incentive programs
*Experience assisting in supervising and staffing new plant start-up

Professional Experience
Production Supervisor, Dixie Beverage Co., 1997–present
*Supervised production, scheduling, human resources and financial performance of

PASSWORD

Please enter a password that will be easy for you to remember. You will need this
password and your e-mail address to apply for job openings at XYZ Corp. or to edit
your resume in the future.

Password: | xyz123 |

Password: | xyz123 | (Again)

your own web site

Posting your résumé and work samples online

Besides submitting your résumé to a database at a career site, you can also post a version of it on a Web page. For your résumé to be viewed on a career site, an employer generally must register with the site in order to search through its database, but if you post your résumé on a public Web page, anyone can view it.

Of course, in order for someone to actually come across your résumé, they would need to have the Web address for the page. So you are likely to get more of a response from potential employers by having your résumé in a database.

Publishing your résumé on your own Web page allows you to have an enhanced version of your text document to which you can refer employers for additional information. For example, you might e-mail a plain text version of your résumé in response to a job listing but refer hiring managers to your Web site to see samples of your work. Graphic artists, photographers, writers, Web designers, or anyone who would submit a portfolio of their work to a potential employer can benefit from having their résumé and work samples online.

Where to Post Your Résumé on a Web Page

- **Your own Web site**
You can register your own address, like
www.firstnamelastname.com, for a fee of less than $30 a year
(though if you have a common name, someone else may already
have registered it, and you may have to opt for a variation of your
name). Once you have registered an address, you'll still need to
hire a company to host your site—meaning that company is
responsible for displaying your page to users. Your Internet service provider can help you register an address and host your Web
pages, but you can also use a third-party service.

- **Through your Internet service provider**
Many Internet service providers offer users free or inexpensive
ways to set up a Web page within the provider's site. In this case,
your address would be something like **home.earthlink.net/your-
name**—in other words, a subpage within the provider's site.

- **At a career or community Web site**
Sites that maintain résumé databases or offer job listings sometimes allow members to set up a Web page, too. You can also create a Web page at community sites like Yahoo (**www.yahoo.com**).

Don't Mix Personal with Professional

If you do post your résumé on your own Web site, make sure
the rest of the site does not contain information that might
put off potential employers—like a personal journal, photos
from your trip to Barbados, or a description of all the items
you're selling on eBay. It's best to maintain one site that's
purely professional; you never know what detail about your
hobbies or musings might raise a red flag.

online privacy and confidentiality

Use your own judgment

Sometimes when you're conducting a job search you need or want to be discreet—if, for instance, you don't want your current boss to know you're looking for a new job.

Fortunately, most career Web sites have taken that into consideration and have designed their résumé databases with features that protect job seekers' privacy. Typically, these features allow users to hide their names and contact information, and sometimes even the names of current or former employers. (Firms contact someone who has posted a confidential résumé by sending an e-mail to an anonymous address set up by the résumé service; the e-mail is forwarded to the candidate.)

Some résumé services also let job seekers selectively block their résumé from being viewed by certain companies. So, for instance, you can indicate you do not want anyone at your current company to be able to find your résumé if they happen to use the same service to find potential employees. But keep in mind that this option isn't always foolproof; if you're worried about losing your job because your boss might find out you're looking, don't post your résumé online. Instead, seek other ways to network or approach the firm directly.

When you're submitting your résumé to a career site, you'll be presented with more information about options for keeping your résumé private or confidential; be sure to read the details carefully. And don't rely entirely on the career service to keep your job search private. Even when you take advantage of these confidentiality features, it's possible for someone to figure out who you are based on other details in your work experience. If you have a unique background—say, you worked for a bank in Abu Dhabi for two years after college, then moved to Miami to work for an import/export business—someone who knows you may figure out whose résumé they're looking at even if your name isn't listed.

Other Privacy Concerns

While there are advantages to utilizing the Internet for its vast networking potential, there are also some drawbacks. Once you submit your résumé to a database, for example, you no longer have complete control over who sees it.

You may get contacted about job openings at companies you'd never in a million years want to work for. Overly aggressive **recruiters**—professionals paid by companies to find employees—might submit your résumé for a job opening without checking with you first. And if you reveal sensitive personal information when you're posting your résumé, like your salary expectations, you never know who might see it.

Think twice about the information you're posting, and research the policies and reputation of the career service you plan to use before you make the digital leap.

FIRST PERSON DISASTER STORY

Private Time

When I first started using career Web sites, I was panicked about finding a job so I didn't bother reading any of the sites' privacy policies before submitting my résumé to their databases. Was that ever a mistake! One of the services I used turned out to be a shady operation that was just interested in collecting e-mail addresses to sell to junk mail distributors. I finally had to get a new e-mail address because I was getting so many offers for get-rich-quick schemes and other marketing scams. Now, I always research a site and check its privacy policy before handing over any personal data.

Sharon O., Tucson, Arizona

now what do I do?

Answers to common questions

Can I apply for jobs listed on recruiting Web sites without posting my résumé?

Career Web sites have different policies about that. Some sites let you search through their job listings without posting your résumé or even becoming a member. (In that case, you just apply for jobs using the contact information the employer has listed.) Other sites will not let you view job postings without registering or submitting your résumé.

Is it okay to send just a cover letter and link to the résumé posted on my own Web site?

Employers may not bother clicking the link to visit your Web site; it's also possible your site could be having technical difficulties when someone tries to visit. Your safest bet is to include a copy of your résumé with your cover letter; you can still include a link to your Web site and let employers know that they can find more information or samples of your work there.

How do I know what happens to my résumé once I submit it to a database?

If you've submitted it through the Web site of an employer—i.e., applied for a job directly—you may or may not get an e-mail message acknowledging the receipt of your résumé. (That's also the case when you apply for a job via e-mail; although it's not technically difficult for employers to send an automated response, many don't bother.) Some career Web sites that maintain résumé databases will track how often your résumé has been viewed. Since Internet technology changes constantly, these tracking systems are likely to get more and more sophisticated, providing both employers and job seekers with better tools.

How can I target my résumé to each job if I submit just one version to a résumé database?

Even if your résumé is in a database at a career site, you don't necessarily have to use that version to reply to a job posting. Some sites give you a choice when you apply for jobs: You can use the version of your résumé in their database or e-mail your résumé directly (and thus tailor it to a particular opening). Also, some companies allow you to update your résumé after submitting it to a database, so another option is to revise the online version before applying for a job.

Will I seem overeager if I drop off my résumé in person?

Not necessarily, although if you make a nuisance of yourself—say, by insisting on handing it to the hiring manager personally—your résumé may end up in the trash instead of at the top of the pile. If you deliver your résumé, make sure any impression you leave with it is a positive one: professional and courteous.

I've spent months surfing job boards and applying for jobs online without a single response. What am I doing wrong?

You may need to try other approaches. While the Internet can be a great resource for job listings, it should not be your only method of searching for a job. Because it is often easier to submit a résumé online, job board postings tend to bring in hundreds of résumés—often overwhelming hiring managers. Try more traditional approaches, such as networking and making cold calls to hiring managers at firms most likely to need someone with your skills.

Now where do I go?

WEB SITES

Post your résumé and search through job listings at:

Monster
www.monster.com

HotJobs
www.hotjobs.com

CareerBuilder
www.careerbuilder.com
Specializes in media companies.

America's Job Bank
www.ajb.org
Specializes in federal and state employment.

Dice
www.dice.com
For technology professionals.

BOOKS

The Everything Online Job Search Book
by Steven Graber
A guide to sites where you can post your résumé, network online, and research employers.

For lists of recruiters by industry, geography, and specialty, see:

The Directory of Executive Recruiters 2003
by Kennedy Information

The Global 200 Executive Recruiters: An Essential Guide to the Best Recruiters in the United States, Europe, Asia, and Latin America
by Nancy Garrison-Jenn

Revising and updating

Take some time and create several different résumés and cover letters that will work for various types of jobs.

one is not enough

Don't take the easy way out

Great, you now have a terrific résumé and cover letter. Now, of course, you could mail out the same résumé and cover letter to a whole variety of jobs and see what happens. Or you could take some time and create several different résumés and cover letters that will work for the various types of jobs you are interested in (marketing vs. sales) or the different types of companies (large firms vs. small ones).

Or you could be even more proactive in your job search and revise your résumé and cover letter each and every time you apply for a job. Think about it. By not revising your paperwork you are sending the job-search equivalent of the junk mail that crowds your own mailbox—one size fits all—and employers will have the same reaction you do to yet another credit card offer: They'll toss it aside.

That said, revising your résumé does not mean you have to start from scratch. Start with a template—either the most recent version of your résumé or one you sent for a similar job opening. For instance, if you recently applied for a position as a graphic designer and another position as a photo editor, pick the résumé that best fits the job you're applying for now and revise it as necessary.

Revising vs. Updating

There's a difference between revising your résumé—tweaking it to make it appealing to a different employer—and updating your résumé after it has been gathering digital dust on your computer's hard drive. Revising is like adding a new exercise to your daily gym workout; updating is like devising a whole new workout regimen.

ASK THE EXPERTS

I wrote a great cover letter for a job listing. Can I just make a few changes and use it again?

Once you've written a good cover letter, it can be tempting to use it again and again. But ideally, you should write a new cover letter each time you send your résumé out. As e-mail has replaced paper in the job search process, cover letters have gotten much shorter and to the point, so it's rare that you would be able to reuse a note you sent someone about a different job.

However, you can use phrases or sentences you've already written as a guideline or a way to overcome the anxiety of a blank page or screen. But don't resort to a Mad Lib–style cover letter (see sample, page 185). Something generic may be easy to revise, but it won't impress your reader. Ultimately, it's better to spend more time writing fewer cover letters than to blast out hundreds of letters that don't generate any response.

Can I update my résumé after sending it to a recruiter?

Usually, recruiters don't mind if you send an updated version of your résumé, but they might get irritated if a new copy arrives every week. Send a new version when you have something significant to add, not every time you change a few words.

sample cover letters

Tailor your cover
letter to the job

Customized Cover Letter

Dear Mrs. Giannovi:

I read Good & Prentis' classified ad for an associate account executive in Sunday's *New York Times* and am writing to apply for the position. I have more than two years of experience as an assistant account executive at Broome & Berg Public Relations, where I've worked on a wide array of accounts with a diversified group of clients.

I know that your firm specializes in the consumer electronics industry, and I think my exposure to my current company's clients in that sector would make me a perfect candidate for this position. I have played an important role for many of these clients, both in terms of press events at industry conventions and organizing interviews and reviews with major media outlets. These experiences have put me in a wonderful position to make a real impact in the position you are advertising.

As you'll see from my résumé, I graduated from Tufts with a dual degree in English and business communications, and after graduating I spent a full year as a paid intern working for Alabaster Public Relations, which is located in San Diego, California. That position opened my eyes to the exciting world of public relations and I haven't been the same since then. My former supervisor at Alabaster, Kevin Masters, would be pleased to speak with you if you have any questions about my performance or abilities.

I am very interested in the associate account executive position you are advertising and would like to learn more about it. Please review my enclosed résumé and let me know if you have any questions. I look forward to hearing from you soon.

Sincerely,

Noelle Cangelosi

Noelle Cangelosi

Generic Cover Letter

To Whom It May Concern:

I read your advertisement for an associate account executive in Sunday's *New York Times* and am writing to apply for the position. I have more than two years of experience as an assistant account executive at Broome & Berg Public Relations, where I've worked on a wide array of accounts with a diversified group of clients. I have played an important role in many client meetings, press events, media interviews, and brainstorming sessions, and I think that with my skills and experience, I could make an immediate impact as part of your company.

I graduated from Tufts with a dual degree in English and business communications, and I spent a full year after graduating as a paid intern working for Alabaster Public Relations, located in San Diego, California.

I am very interested in the job you are advertising and would like to learn more about it. Please review my résumé and let me know if you have any questions. I look forward to hearing from you soon.

Sincerely,

Noelle Cangelosi

Noelle Cangelosi

archive systems

As you apply for jobs, send out networking letters, and follow up with thank-you notes, it's a good idea to create a paper or electronic filing system to keep track of your job search. That way, if someone calls you for an interview, you'll know which version of your résumé you sent to the company (and you can make sure you bring the same copy when you show up at the office). You'll also want a calendar with a "to do" list so that when you send an e-mail message promising to follow up with a phone call in a few days, you won't forget to make the call.

To keep accurate records of your search:

■ Create a folder for every company you contact, either on your computer or using plain old paper envelopes or folders.

■ Save a copy of each letter and résumé you send, plus a copy of the job advertisement (if there was one) and any background information you have about the employer. Keep this information in one place so it's easy to find later on.

FIRST PERSON SUCCESS STORY

Paper Trail

In my last job search, I sent out so many résumés that when I finally got a phone call from a company interested in setting up an interview I had trouble remembering what the job opening was. Luckily, I had saved a copy of each résumé and cover letter I sent, along with the classified ad describing the position and any information I could find about the company. Within minutes of getting the call, I started reading my notes about the company and doing an online search for more information. My interview was slated for the next morning and I am pretty sure that having that information on hand helped me land the job.

Peter W., Albany, New York

■ On your computer, save each résumé and cover letter using a name that will remind you of the recipient, like MicrosoftResume or GeneralElectricCoverLtr. It's also helpful to include the date, e.g., AvonResume12-02-02.

■ Make a list of the people or companies you have contacted, whether you heard back, and when you followed up. Be sure to note the people you talked to (or wrote) as well as their e-mail addresses and phone numbers.

■ If you have promised to get in touch with someone, mark your calendar so you don't forget to send an e-mail or call.

■ Keep track of the Web sites where you submit your résumé online—and print out copies of each résumé you post. Be sure to update your online résumé if several months have passed or you have additional experience to add (see page 188).

■ Create a folder in your e-mail inbox for messages related to your job search. Be sure to transfer any relevant incoming messages to this folder as well as the messages you send out. (Check your e-mail program's Help section for instructions on creating folders.)

revising your résumé

Tailoring your submission

There are no strict guidelines about what you should revise on your résumé, because each scenario is different and what you start with may be more or less appropriate for a particular job. For instance, if you've been working as a lawyer and are hoping to change careers, you'll have more work to do than someone who is simply looking to change law firms. Here are some questions to ask yourself before you send out your résumé.

■ **What's your objective?**
Tailor your objective to the situation. If you're applying for a specific job, change your objective to loosely match the job title, e.g., "A position as a pharmaceutical sales representative." If you're sending your résumé to a recruiter, use a broader objective, such as "A position in business development or sales."

■ **Is your summary targeted to a particular company or job?**
Revise your Summary of Qualifications so it highlights the skills mentioned as requirements for the position, e.g., "10 years of experience as a travel agent," if the ad is for a travel industry professional. You might want to delete this section from your résumé if you are making the same points in your cover letter—especially if you are sending your résumé by e-mail, since recipients have less patience for redundancy when reading online.

■ **Do you have any new experience to add?**
If you're updating your résumé after some time has passed, you probably have some new experience to add, like a new job, recent accomplishments at your current job, or something you have done while on a hiatus from work. It may also be time to delete older jobs, particularly if your résumé is more than a page long.

■ Are you highlighting the right skills?

Make sure your work experience emphasizes accomplishments that are relevant to the position you are applying for or the company you are targeting. That means one version of your résumé might highlight your fund-raising experience while another focuses on your management skills.

■ Should you use a different format?

If you've been using a functional résumé and aren't getting many responses, consider trying a chronological format (see page 14).

■ Should you relocate your education section?

If you're a not-so-recent college graduate, it may be time to move this section to the bottom of your résumé, but if you just got an advanced degree, you may want to move your education higher up.

■ Is your contact information up-to-date?

If you've moved or switched e-mail addresses, be sure to update your résumé. You don't want to lose a job opportunity because an employer couldn't reach you.

■ Did you recheck your spelling and grammar?

Don't forget to check for spelling or grammatical errors each time you make changes on your résumé; that extra minute or two could save you from an embarrassing typo.

troubleshooting

If you've been looking for a job for a long time and haven't gotten many responses, it may be time to revise your résumé. This type of revision, or retooling, is sometimes necessary when something simply isn't working.

Take a look at the questions on the opposite page or revisit the first five chapters and see if there are any areas you still need to work on. It may also help to enlist a friend or colleague to look at your résumé and give you feedback; choose someone whose advice you value, and be open to constructive criticism.

In some cases, it's worthwhile to hire a professional résumé writer or career counselor to help you with your résumé. You can usually find these professionals in the phone book; look under "résumé" or "career" in the yellow pages, but be sure to ask for references and research the service before spending any money. You can also find help online by searching for "résumé" and "service."

Your résumé may not be the problem

Even if you aren't getting the response you want, it may have nothing to do with your résumé or cover letter—especially in a tight job market. These documents are just one aspect of your search; your networking abilities, work experience, job targets, and career goals all affect how long it will take you to find a job. You may need to focus on these other areas if your search has dragged on. For example, you may want to expand your job targets or desired geographical location.

If You're Not Getting a Response ...

■ **Is your résumé too long?** If your résumé is more than one page, try trimming it down.

■ **Do you have a clear objective?** Is your objective overly broad—or have you left this section out? You may need to clarify your objective so employers know what you want.

■ **Do your accomplishments support your objective?** Make sure the skills and achievements you list are relevant to the job you want. Having met your sales goals three years in a row is impressive, but that's not what an employer is interested in if you're applying for a teaching job.

■ **Are your descriptions too wordy or dense?** It's critical that your résumé be easy to read. Eliminate long sentences or use bullet points instead of paragraphs of text.

■ **Are you sending your résumé in the right format?** Copy your résumé into the body of an e-mail message in addition to—or instead of—sending it as an attachment.

■ **Have you included enough keywords** (the words employers enter into search fields to find appropriate résumés)? Employers may not come across your résumé if it's in a database and you haven't included enough, or the right, keywords (see page 112).

■ **Is there a "red flag" in your résumé?** There may be an issue with your résumé you've overlooked—a gap in your work history, for instance, or too many jobs. See Chapter 4 for advice on dealing with résumé problems.

■ **Are there any typos?** One misspelled word or a single grammar mistake might disqualify you from consideration—even if your experience is top-notch.

■ **Have you followed up with a phone call or e-mail?** Don't call to ask, "Did you get my résumé," but a polite inquiry about the status of the hiring process can open the door to further conversation.

are you overqualified?

Employers may
think you're too
good for the job

Sometimes the problem with a résumé is not that it's poorly written or badly organized—it may be that it's too good. Or rather, the person applying for the position may be overqualified.

Particularly in a tight job market, when many qualified candidates are competing for fewer positions, job seekers often apply for openings that require less experience than they have. But hiring managers have a tendency to skip over résumés from candidates who appear overqualified, on the theory that someone with more experience than necessary will be unhappy in the position or jump ship when the job market picks up.

If you find yourself in this situation—for economic reasons or because you're trying to change careers—you may need to pare down your résumé before sending it out. Revising your résumé to fit, but not exceed, the requirements of the position can help you land an interview.

Once you get your foot in the door, you can decide for yourself whether it's a job you want. Companies have valid reasons for not hiring employees who are overqualified; you'll need to be certain you're willing to take a pay cut or accept less responsibility before you head down this road.

How to Make Your Résumé Less Intimidating

■ **Ditch your degree.**
If you have an M.B.A., Ph.D., or other advanced degree that isn't required for the position you want, it may be to your advantage to leave it off your résumé. Some managers are reluctant to hire applicants who appear smarter than they themselves are, out of fear such employees would go after their jobs.

■ **Deflate your job titles.**
If you were president of a small company and are applying for a position lower in the hierarchy of a big corporation, consider revising your previous job title. Whenever you apply for a position that seems like you're taking a step down, employers may doubt that you'll really settle for a smaller role. By taking the pomp out of a fancy job title, you can eliminate that concern and after an interview with the prospective boss, judge for yourself whether you're willing to take a step down.

■ **Downplay your experience.**
If you managed a budget of $5 million in your last position and are applying for a job where you'd be responsible for a budget of $500,000, it's a good idea to leave earlier numbers out of your résumé, or say something vague, like "more than a million dollars." The same goes for other details that make you seem too experienced.

■ **Delete less recent jobs.**
If your age is the issue (see page 92), consider deleting some previous work experience from your résumé. If an opening requires 5 years of experience and you have 10 to 15, leaving out an older job or two can put you in the zone the employer is targeting.

paring down a résumé

An overqualified résumé before and after editing

There are times—such as when you are re-entering the job market after holding a lofty post at a young age or running your own firm—when you may need to downplay some of your accomplishments.

1. By carefully editing your résumé, removing intimidating titles you have held or accolades you collected, you will make yourself a more approachable job candidate.

2. Consider removing revenue or budget figures that might make you seem out of reach for a smaller firm.

3. If you hold an advanced degree that is not required for the post you are applying for, remove it from your résumé.

Original Résumé

Fred F. Seidenberg
frcd_seidenberg@abi.com
150 West Seventh Street
Cincinnati, Ohio 45202
Telephone: 513-555-8985 Fax: 513-555-2934

PROFESSIONAL CAREER
American Brands International, 2002 to present, ~~Founder and~~ President
•~~Launched and ran~~ consumer products company that produced and distributed health care products to retail companies nationwide
•Developed prototypes, directed manufacturing, and managed marketing and sales team
•~~Built company from start-up operation to 25-employee firm with more than $1 million in annual revenues~~

BNR Vitamins Inc., 1988–2002, Vice President, Sales
•Forecasted sales and production volumes for this international manufacturer and distributor of vitamins
•Directed sales team in marketing and selling product line to nationwide retail accounts, ~~representing $200 million in annual sales~~
•Worked with marketing department to design packaging, promotional materials, and ~~$800,000~~ advertising program, including television, radio, and print media

Thomson Health Company, 1984–1988, Sales and Marketing Director
•~~Managed $200,000 sales budget~~
•Assigned sales quota for 25 regional managers
•Designed telemarketing, direct mail, and partnership marketing campaigns prospecting for new business

GN Company, 1982–1984, National Account Representative
•Handled 20 national retail accounts ~~representing $20 million in annual sales~~, boosting annual sales by 10 percent on average
•Delivered 10 major new accounts
•Rated top salesperson

~~PUBLICATIONS~~
~~*International Business* (Aries Books, Chicago, 1998)~~
~~Multiple articles on global business & corporate governance~~

EDUCATION
Carnegie Mellon University, M.B.A.
~~U.S. Naval Language School, Chinese~~
University of Pennsylvania, B.S.
~~Noble American Graduate School of International Business, Doctor of International Law (Honorary)~~

194

Fred F. Seidenberg
fred_seidenberg@webmail.net
150 West Seventh Street
Cincinnati, Ohio 54321
Telephone: 513-555-8985 Fax: 513-555-2934

PROFESSIONAL CAREER

American Brands International, 2002 to present, President
• Managed consumer products company that produced and distributed health care products to retail companies nationwide
• Developed prototypes, directed manufacturing, and managed marketing and sales team

BNR Vitamins Inc., 1988–2002, Vice President, Sales
• Forecasted sales and production volumes for this international manufacturer and distributor of vitamins
• Directed sales team in marketing and selling product line to nationwide retail accounts
• Worked with marketing department to design packaging, promotional materials, and advertising program, including television, radio, and print media

Thomson Health Company, 1984–1988, Sales and Marketing Director
• Assigned sales quota for 25 regional managers
• Designed telemarkcting, direct mail, and partnership marketing campaigns prospecting for new business

GN Company, 1982–1984, National Account Representative
• Handled 20 national retail accounts, boosting annual sales by 10 percent on average
• Delivered 10 major new accounts
• Rated top salesperson

EDUCATION
Carnegie Mellon University, M.B.A.
University of Pennsylvania, B.S.

updating your
résumé online

Polish your qualifications

After you have posted your résumé on a career or recruiting Web site (see page 110), you can almost always go back and revise it later on. It's a good idea to do this from time to time—not only does it give you the chance to update your information, but at some sites it keeps your résumé from fading into electronic oblivion.

The best source for advice on updating and polishing your online résumé is probably the career site itself. Each service works a little differently, but most have Help sections with pages of tips on building your online résumé and improving its chances of showing up in the search results when employers use the site to find candidates.

Some services even let users view statistics on how often their résumé has been "found" in a search by employers, and how many times the résumé was actually viewed. If your résumé is not being seen, that could be a clue that you need to add more keywords (see page 112), give your résumé a catchier title, or work on polishing your qualifications.

The problem may also be a simple mistake; you may have inadvertently "hidden" your résumé from view or forgotten to activate it after you entered your information. Many career sites have message boards where you can post questions if you need help, or in some cases a phone number you can call.

ASK THE EXPERTS

I posted my résumé on a site that allows members to pay a fee to improve their résumé's visibility in employers' search results. Is that something I should consider?

In exchange for a fee, some résumé databases now offer job seekers preferential placement in the results listings when employers search for résumés. Whether it's worth paying such a fee is up to you, but read the fine print carefully before you offer up your credit card.

I posted my résumé on a career Web site but can't remember my password. Can I still update my résumé?

Most career sites have a feature to help users who have forgotten their password. When you first registered as a member, you may have given a password hint the site can e-mail back to you, like your favorite color. If you don't see a link on the site that says something like "Forgot your password?" look in the Help section.

I submitted my résumé to an employer's Web site instead of a career site. Can I still update it?

Some companies that accept résumés online offer a way for job seekers to update their information, but some don't. If the site you're on doesn't allow updates, you can try e-mailing the human resources contact and asking for help—or simply resubmit an updated version of your résumé.

now what do I do?

Answers to common questions

I sent an e-mail about my job search to a former colleague but never heard back. Should I resend the same message or write a new one?

It's probably best to write a new message and tactfully mention your earlier note. Or try giving the recipient a call—sometimes an e-mail can pave the way for making a connection by phone. But resending the first e-mail might seem like a subtle reprimand to the recipient for not responding—or you may have written something the first time that was a turnoff. Try a new angle and see what happens.

I got a call for an interview and can't remember which version of my résumé I sent the company. Is it okay to ask them to send me a copy?

That's probably not a great idea. It makes you sound disorganized and could be taken as a sign that you stretched the truth about your experience—and need to be reminded about what you included on your résumé. Better to show up for the interview with a new version and say you've updated the one you sent earlier.

I had to get a new e-mail address, but the old one is on dozens of résumés I've sent out. Should I contact those companies to give them my new information?

Most likely, employers will call you if they're interested in setting up an interview. But if you're worried they'll try e-mail first, see if the company that gave you your old e-mail address will forward your mail to a new one. (They may charge a small fee for this service.) If that doesn't set your mind at ease, contact the employers who have your résumé on file and let them know your new address.

I've heard it's a good idea to update a résumé you've posted online because then it will be at the top of the list when employers search for job candidates. Is that true?

It depends on where you have posted your résumé. Some sites do treat new résumés and those that have been updated recently differently than résumés that have been in their database for a while. Check the site's policies and see if they recommend returning every few weeks to update your information. It may increase the chance that your résumé will be viewed by potential employers.

Now where do I go?

WEB SITES

www.resume.com
Résumé writing service.

Job listings and career advice:

www.monster.com

www.hotjobs.com

www.careerbuilder.com

BOOKS

Damn Good Résumé Catalog: A Crash Course in Résumé Writing
by Yana Parker

Don't Send a Résumé: And Other Contrarian Rules to Help Land a Great Job
by Jeffrey J. Fox

How to Say It in Your Job Search
by Robbie Kaplan

glossary

Action verbs Active verbs, such as "developed," "persuaded," or "motivated," that express action and can be used to dynamically describe work experience.

Affiliations A résumé section where a candidate lists memberships in professional organizations.

Age Discrimination in Employment Act Passed in 1978, this federal law prohibits employers from discriminating against people age 40 or over. In some states, this age is as young as 18.

Archive system A paper or electronic filing system used to keep track of your job search.

Career counselors People who are qualified through their credentials and experience to use various psychological tools to help you figure out which jobs suit your interests and talents.

Chronological résumé A résumé that lists work experience starting with the most recent job and working backward, with specific achievements listed below each position held.

Cold call Also known as a broadcast letter, this term refers to a letter written by a candidate when approaching a firm that is not currently advertising for employees.

Cover letter A letter, submitted with a résumé, that serves as an introduction.

CV Short for the Latin phrase *curriculum vitae*, meaning "life's course," this is a longer alternative to the traditional résumé, offering more detailed information about a candidate's work experience and achievements.

Digital résumé A résumé in an electronic file format, such as a plain text or Microsoft Word document.

Employment agencies These firms fill entry- and midlevel jobs for a number of employers. Do not work with an employment agency that requires you to pay a fee.

Employment gap A brief or long period of time between jobs.

Font A design term referring to the style of letters, or typeface, used in a document.

Functional résumé A résumé organized according to various skills acquired during the candidate's career, with specific accomplishments listed below skills headings (such as "sales" or "project management") instead of below job titles.

Headers The fields that appear at the top of an e-mail message and contain the sender's and recipient's names.

Headhunter A professional placement specialist, also known as a recruiter, hired by companies to screen job candidates for positions.

Hiring manager The person who has the authority to hire you. Often, this is also the person to whom you would directly report once on the job.

Honors & Awards An optional résumé section where a candidate may list distinctions received during his or her career.

Hybrid résumé A résumé that combines features of the chronological and functional résumé formats.

Job database A Web site that posts job listings from employers as well as résumés of people seeking employment.

Job objective A sentence or phrase detailing what type of job you are looking for.

Keywords Words or phrases like "sales manager" "editor," or "banking" that describe job qualifications. Employers may use computers to scan résumé databases for keywords to identify possible job candidates.

Linear résumé A résumé format in which jobs are listed in chronological order, beginning with the most recent, and bulleted phrases appear below each job description.

Margins The white space between the text and the edges of the page.

Networking cover letter A letter written to your contacts—friends, relatives, former co-workers—requesting advice or information.

Online application form An application form, also known as a résumé builder, posted on a company or career Web site that job seekers are asked to fill out.

Optical character recognition (OCR) technology Technology used to convert paper documents into electronic files for storage in a computer database.

Professional résumé A shortened version of the CV often used by medical or legal professionals.

Profile A résumé section, also known as a Summary of Qualifications or Skills Summary, where a candidate details specific skills acquired during his or her career.

Publications & Presentations An optional résumé section where candidates may list professional presentations and/or books or papers published.

Recruiter A professional placement specialist, also known as a headhunter, hired by companies to screen job candidates for open positions.

Résumé A one- to two-page document that details your educational and professional experiences. It can also include lists of publications, awards, professional association memberships, and specific skills.

Résumé builder An electronic form on a potential employer's Web site that job seekers can fill out to apply for open positions.

Résumé database The electronic equivalent of a filing cabinet where résumés are stored on either a career or company Web site. Hiring managers can search for appropriate résumés using keywords.

Sans serif A type of font, or typeface, with letters made of simple lines.

Serif A type of font, or typeface, in which letters have little flourishes where the lines end; the preferred style for résumés.

Scanner A device used to create an electronic image of a paper document.

Summary of Qualifications A résumé section, also known as a Profile or Skills Summary, where a candidate details specific skills acquired during his or her career.

Transferable skills Skills you've developed in past jobs that you "carry with" you into the next job, such as skills in project management, public speaking, or team leadership.

Typeface A design term referring to the style of letters, or the font, used in a document.

White space Blank areas on a résumé that separate blocks of information.

Widows A copyediting term for places in a document where a single word or two spills over to the last line of a paragraph or section of text.

index

Barnes & Noble Books
is pleased to present **Business Basics**.
This ground breaking series was designed with your business needs in mind
and contains clear, concise information on key subjects close to your heart.
You'll find smart, inside information on personal budgeting,
writing job-winning resumes, and starting your own business.
Barnes & Noble Business Basics:
Résumés and Cover Letters
Personal Budgeting
Starting a Business
Getting a Grant

About the Author

Susan Stellin is a freelance writer living in New York City. She has written about business, career, and workplace issues for the *New York Times* and other publications, and has interviewed many career advisors and managers about what it takes to land a job—both in a booming and a challenging economy. Previously, she worked at the *New York Times* on the Web and San Francisco–based CNET Networks, editing articles about the Internet and technology.

Barnes & Noble Business Basics *Résumés and Cover Letters*
Barbara J. Morgan Publisher
Barb Chintz Editorial Director
Leonard Vigliarolo Design Director
Jennifer Pellet Editor
Elizabeth McNulty Editorial Production Coordinator
Leslie Stem Design Assistant
Emily Seese Editorial Assistant
Della R. Mancuso Production Manager

Barnes & Noble Books would like to thank the following consultants for their help in preparing this book:

Ruth K. Robbins of Career Momentum/Résumés Plus in New York City, and a certified counselor of the Five O' Clock Club; and

Colleen Stewart, an executive recruiter in Atlanta, Georgia.

Photo Credits All illustrations courtesy of **Artville** except the following: **digitalvision** 3, 38, 43, 68, 82, 85, 88, 152, 154, 162, 165, 176; **Rubberball** (headshots) 7, 29, 33, 55, 75, 97, 119, 143, 161, 181